Steam

Tales from the Footplate

Colin G. Maggs

SUTTON PUBLISHING

First published in the United Kingdom in 1999
Sutton Publishing Limited · Phoenix Mill · Stroud · Gloucestershire

Paperback edition first published in 2001

British Library Cataloguing-in-Publication Data.
A record for this book is available from the British Library.

ISBN 0-7509-2740-2

Typeset in 11/13pt Bembo.
Typesetting and origination by
Sutton Publishing Limited.
Printed and bound in Great Britain by
J.H. Haynes & Co., Sparkford.

Contents

INTRODUCTION

Most footplatemen take great pleasure in talking about their job and rightly so, for the driver of a steam locomotive enjoys considerable status. He is in charge of hundreds of tons of goods, hundreds of tons of rolling stock and responsible for the lives and safety of several hundred passengers.

Engine driving is not easy. It looks quite simple – you just go round with an oil can squirting a few drops on all moving surfaces, climb on the footplate, blow the whistle, open the regulator and off you go. Similarly, all the fireman seems to do is shovel enough coal into the firebox to generate heat, ensure that the boiler has sufficient water and in his spare time help his driver look out for signals. Highly skilled footplatemen can make their job appear simple, but there is much more to it than meets the eye. A number of things can go wrong and skilled judgement is required to make sure that no one is placed in danger, that the train is not delayed more than absolutely necessary and that other trains are not made late.

I have spent many happy hours listening to railwaymen's stories and have included some of them in this book, having checked as far as possible that the facts are accurate. I gratefully acknowledge the generous and friendly help of railwaymen from Bescot to Bournemouth: R. Adams; J. Barber; J. Beck; C.A.J. Cook; F. Epps; R. Ford; N.C. Gibbons; E. Gray; R. Gray; A. Gunning; T. Gunning; D. Holden; F. Holmes; L.R. Moore; W. Rawles; E. Smith; F. Staddon; J. Stamp; D. Thorne; G. Tucker; R. Weeks and L. West. Particular thanks are also due to R.B. Ireland for checking and improving the text.

Chapter One

CLEANING AND FIRING DUTIES

How old were you when you first wanted to be an engine driver? Although you may well have had this yearning at a very tender age, quite a proportion of those who eventually arrived at that exalted position did so after starting in some other job. The experience of Driver Bob Ford of Bath was quite typical: 'I certainly wasn't mad keen on steam engines and wasn't one who just couldn't wait until I was old enough to leave school, go along to the shed master and get him to put my name down on the waiting list to be a cleaner. As a lad I wasn't particularly interested in locos – I knew they were things that pulled trains and that was the extent of my knowledge and interest.' On leaving school Bob's first job was as a delivery boy pushing a baker's handcart. He then moved on to mechanical transport and drove an 8 horse power Ford van for a different baker until another lad suggested that he should join the railway in order to earn more money.

In his early days Fred Epps, another young Bathonian, was just as unenthusiastic about railways as Bob Ford. Nine months out of work, he went to the Labour Exchange and was told to try for a job on the railway. He was accepted and his pay packet of 30s a week made him feel rich compared with the 8s he had received on the dole.

In 1915 Edgar Gray started on the Midland Railway at Bath aged fifteen. He took the job of his brother, who had enlisted in the Army. Edgar worked a twelve-hour day and was paid about 10s a week. During each twelve-hour session, either 6.00 a.m. to 6.00 p.m., or 6.00 p.m. to 6.00 a.m., he cleaned one engine and also filled coal tubs on the coaling stage. In the days of the Somerset & Dorset, engines were cleaned with tallow, but when the LMS took over the S&D locomotive stock in 1930, the cheaper 'cleaning oil' was substituted which resulted in some workers contracting dermatitis. Cleaning oil, a type of paraffin, was used on both paint and motion.

In 1934 Ron Gray started at Bath as a bar boy, one week working 6.00 a.m. to 2.00 p.m., the next 2.00 p.m. to 10.00 p.m. and the third week 10.00 p.m. to 6.00 a.m. His tasks included cleaning the tube plate, the brick arch and crown stays in the firebox and shovelling ash into the ashpan and raking it away. Before the water softener was installed at Bath, he used a hook to knock lime off the internal surfaces of the boiler. The engine that had headed the Down 'Pines Express' returned from Bournemouth with the 6.40 p.m., arriving Bath at 10.10 p.m. When it came on shed the fire was drawn and the bar boy who started work at 6.00 a.m. went into the smokebox and cleaned the tubes to ensure that the engine of this important train was capable of giving her best performance. He carried out the work with a long, T-shaped scraper and if a tube was completely blocked, freed it with a dart. The bar boy's work completed, the boilersmith checked that the tubes were indeed free of ash and no water was leaking.

Another job undertaken by a bar boy was to replace the fire bars removed by a fireman when he dropped the fire – a much quicker and pleasanter method than lifting the fire out using a shovel with a 9-ft-long handle. The practice of dropping a fire by lifting the fire bars was started during the Second World War because if the fire had been thrown out through the cab side it might have been seen by hostile aircraft. Therefore to assist in maintaining the blackout all fire was dropped through the ashpan. After the war this practice continued at Bath until closure, although many other depots reverted to

S&DJR 4–4–0 No. 71 in blue livery at Bath locomotive depot with male and female cleaners. A coal stack is
to the left of the smokebox and Messrs Stothert & Pitt's crane works are beyond.

c. 1916 Author's collection

throwing the fire out. Replacing the bars was quite an art. First the bars to be reinserted
were placed almost level with the existing bars; then, with a special iron, a fire bar was
raised vertically and dropped into position. Each bar was done in turn. If a boy miscued,
the bar clanged down into the ashpan and he had to go underneath the engine and
recover it.

Shovelling char from a smokebox was unpleasant, not only because it was dusty and
dirty, but also because of the choking sulphur fumes released. Very often on engines that
had come from the north, char reached up to the top of the blast pipe because it had not
been emptied as often as it should have been. Bath men believed that in the 'North' (as
Bath men called the Midlands), the men were either too tired or too lazy to do it.
Apparently the men there would open a smokebox door, craftily let some char drop out
on the front of the engine to make it appear as if it had all been shovelled out, and then
close the door again leaving most of the char still inside. It is probable that at a big shed

The smokebox of Class 5 4–6–0 No. 45065 is receiving attention at Nuneaton depot.

13.9.65 Revd Alan Newman

such as Saltley, stabling about 200 engines, those in charge found it difficult to maintain checks on such activities.

If char was left in, when it rose to a certain height it blocked the firetubes and the consequent lack of draught gave rise to poor steaming. Some modern depots had a pneumatic apparatus – similar to a giant vacuum cleaner – for emptying smokeboxes. Just after the Second World War some 'Black Fives' were equipped with a small steam valve. When this was opened towards the end of a journey, a jet of steam disturbed the char, which was then ejected through the chimney by the blast of used steam from the cylinders. The experiment did not continue for long because of complaints received from adjacent landowners about the debris falling on their property. The final solution to this problem was self-cleaning smokeboxes. These had large wire grids that broke the char into small particles which were then thrown out by the blast. Engines fitted with this device had 'SC' marked on their smokeboxes.

When you were aged eighteen you were eligible to become a cleaner, although this job was not necessarily permanent. In December 1920 Fred Holmes started work as a

BR Standard Class 5 4–6–0 No. 73082 *Camelot* of 70A, Nine Elms, shed. Notice the 'SC' (self-cleaning) plate near the foot of the smokebox door. A named Class 5 was rare at Bath.

27.3.64 Revd Alan Newman

Reg Buckley cleaning a Class 4P Compound at Gloucester.

c. 1950 Author's collection

cleaner at Stoke-on-Trent on the North Staffordshire Railway. One subsequent winter he was made redundant and then taken on again when traffic picked up during the summer. In total he was made redundant three times before moving to Bath and becoming a fireman. Sometimes you were given the option of moving to another shed in order to avoid being made redundant. For example, sheds in the Midlands were usually busier in the winter when more coal was required and Bath shed more active in summer when more passenger trains were run.

When moving to another shed, the youths' lodgings were not always home from home. Fred Epps was one of six lads who went to Bescot from Bath one autumn. His lodgings were terrible as they were a long walk from the shed and his evening meal consisted of one slice of bread and butter, a stick of celery, one tomato and a cake – quite insufficient for a hard-working fireman. Another lad from Bath, hearing of Fred's plight, said that he himself was given excellent food, talked to his landlady and Fred happily moved in.

Norman Gibbons started in 1923 as a call boy, an alternative route to becoming a driver. The call boy played an essential role in the days before time checks on the radio and when homes may have only had one timepiece. At night boys called a driver,

S. & D. F. 113
A 4—5/24.

Southern and London Midland and Scottish Railway Companies
SOMERSET AND DORSET JOINT LINE
LOCO. DEPT.
MEN TO CALL.

TRAIN.	NAME.
To commence	
2pm	D. C. Gibbons
Monday 2nd	56 Claude Av
	May 2nd 1927

Time left Shed.................... m.
„ returned .... m.

A call boy's 'calling ticket' used on this occasion for his address.

Author's collection

A scene at Bescot MPD with Class 2P 4–4–0 No. 40646 of 21B (Bourneville); Class 2F 0–6–0 No. 58185

and Class 2MT No. 46427. The ash plant stands on the left.

26.4.62 Revd Alan Newman

fireman and guard an hour before they were due to sign on. The men acknowledged the call, though sometimes they were already up. At Bath, calling was confined to those living south of the River Avon, the railway company thus avoiding the payment of toll-bridge charges. Boys advised drivers on the north side of the river if their duty changed, but would not 'knock them up'. Until about 1930, when the LMS provided a red bicycle for a call boy, he had to visit the sixty or so men on foot. Despite call boys, some men found it hard to get up. One young fireman turned up at 4.00 a.m., half asleep and wearing different coloured socks and pyjama trousers under his overalls. Apparently his mother always had to rouse him.

At one time Guard Frank Staddon lived at 12 Edward Street, Bath. When he arrived at work one morning, he was told that Control would not let him sign on, claiming that the call boy had visited him three times and on each occasion Frank had failed to answer. Frank denied this and said no one had called. Control relented, let him work, but said it must not happen again. When he returned home later that day, Mr Smith at 2 Edward Street told Frank that during the night vandals had kicked his door and it bore the marks of a hob-nailed boot. Frank asked Mr Smith to write a letter to the LMS claiming compensation for damage to his door and for being unnecessarily roused. This letter, of course, vindicated the truth of Frank's statement that the call boy had not paid a visit to him. The reason the call boy went to the wrong house was that the figure '1' on his sheet was indistinct.

As a result of economies, call boys were dispensed with in about 1946. During the winter of 1926 Norman Gibbons was shocked to receive a notice signed by R.C. Archbutt, Locomotive Superintendent, Highbridge, stating 'Your services are no longer required due to slackness in traffic'. He was given a job at Highbridge shed and lodged in the town until the spring when he was able to return to his call boy job at Bath.

Ray Adams started work at Bath as a cleaner in June 1937 and then in the autumn, due to a fall in the seasonal traffic, he and five other junior cleaners went to Gloucester rather than become redundant. The extra coal traffic at that time of the year made Gloucester busier. There he paid 25s per week for lodgings. When Ray was firing, rather than cleaning, he was paid 57s, instead of 34s a week. Before a cleaner could act as a fireman he was required to be able to name the principal parts of a locomotive, know the relevant rules and regulations and be familiar with a fireman's duties and responsibilities. These included seeing that sufficient coal and water were available, the lamps were in working order and the tools correctly positioned. He had to fire his engine to maintain steam, keep a lookout for every signal and was at the beck and call of his driver. Before going off duty, if his engine was returned to shed, he was required to dispose of it by dropping the fire and cleaning out the smokebox.

Ray applied for a transfer back to Bath. This was against the advice of most of his mates, who believed it was financially advantageous to remain at Gloucester where he would have soon achieved his 328 firing days. (When you had fired for 328 days you were paid at the firing rate of 57s a week regardless of whether you were firing or cleaning.) As the Bath depot was only busy in summer, some Bath passed cleaners moved for the winter to Walsall or Kentish Town to get more firing turns. At Bath Ray put in

Guard Frank Staddon, left, and Guard Jack Lake, right, at Bath Midland goods yard.

c. 1960 Author's collection

Class 2P 4–4–0 No. 40540 of 22B (Gloucester) and Class 3F 0–6–0 No. 43599 outside Gloucester shed.
9.8.56 Revd Alan Newman

about 150 days firing in the summer half of the year, so it took him about two years to accumulate 328 days.

Meanwhile, in the autumn of 1938 Ray was made redundant at Bath and received 18s dole money and 12s 6d from the Associated Society of Locomotive Engineers and Firemen, though the latter only paid this rate for three months, after which it fell to 6s a week. Ray obtained a job at a local engineering factory checking the size of shell cases. For this he received only £2 a week, including a monthly bonus, and the job entailed working a twelve-hour day, comparing poorly with his eight-hour day when firing or cleaning. In March 1939 the LMS sent for him because drivers took their holidays between March and September and other men were required to replace those on vacation, as well as to work extra trains. The holiday months allocated to drivers were rotated over the years so that if a driver was given March – a bad month for a holiday – one year, he might be given July the following year.

A memo from Harold Whitaker, District Locomotive Superintendent, to Passed Cleaner Gibbons explaining how he can obtain a transfer.

Author's collection

For a fireman to become a passed fireman he was required to take an examination consisting of about four days of tests. He learned in his own time at mutual improvement classes taken by senior footplatemen in their own time. A fireman had to pass an exam that required him to name every part of an engine and be able to take down one side of the motion, so that if a locomotive became disabled it could be put into a condition that would allow it to be worked back to a shed. This is the great advantage of a steam, over a diesel, engine. When a diesel engine fails, the chances are that nothing can be done out on the road, whereas a steam engine can usually be nursed back to a depot. A fireman was also tested on his knowledge of signalling; rules and regulations; making out reports; oiling and his ability to change a water gauge glass. He was allowed three attempts at this exam and if he failed a third time he was not allowed to go on firing, but was taken off the footplate and put on labouring – but as one driver put it, 'You had to be pretty dim to fail.'

An example of a steam engine still being able to move its train when damaged occurred was when Jack Barber was firing the 9.23 a.m. freight from Bath to Westerleigh. Near

Fireman Morphet at Hellifield shed with a 'scoop' – the name of the large shovel provided by the Midland Railway. No. 456 is a Class 2P 4–4–0.

c. 1920 Author's collection

Bitton station he heard a roar and bang at the front end. Driver Harold Burford walked round the Class 4F 0–6–0 but could see nothing amiss. They proceeded slowly but the engine seemed to lift on one side. They managed to clear Mangotsfield South Junction and leave the road free for the Bath to Bristol stopping train following them. They halted at Mangotsfield North Junction to make another inspection and discovered a nut on the piston rod had become unscrewed. This nut had shattered the cylinder head and from Bitton the engine had largely worked on just one piston. Mangotsfield was remembered by railwaymen because if they worked a train into Carson's chocolate factory sidings, they were allowed to purchase chocolates at a reduced price. This privilege was eventually withdrawn when some men bought too many and sold them to their workmates.

LMS engines at Bath generally used North coal, this being obtained from collieries on

An 890 Class 2–4–0 No. 89 arrives at Bitton station.

c. 1910 M.J. Tozer's collection

that company's system. Although it generally burnt satisfactorily, it gave off a lot of choking sulphureous fumes. This was of little consequence in the open air, but was serious when passing through the 447-yard-long, single-bore Devonshire Tunnel on a rising 1 in 50 gradient out of Bath, and even more serious in the 1,829-yard-long Combe Down Tunnel with a rising gradient of 1 in 100 towards Bath. Conditions were so bad that locomotive crews had to breathe through wet handkerchiefs and on occasions when the fumes were particularly severe, they crouched on the floor where the air was

Ticket to be completed by a driver before signing-off if his engine required 'No Repairs'.

LMS

E.R.O. 23458

Date

Driver

PAY No.

NO REPAIRS

ENG. No.

SHED No.
OF ENG.

Mangotsfield North Junction signal-box, right, and the station building of the original station, left.

21.4.60 Author

Class 4F 0–6–0 No. 4276, shedded at Bristol Barrow Road, on the water tower siding, Mangotsfield. Part of
Carson's chocolate factory can be seen in the background on the left.

30.7.36 Revd Alan Newman

Class 7F 2–8–0 No. 53803 emerges from Devonshire Tunnel with the 11.20 a.m. freight from Bath to Evercreech Junction.

13.11.54 R.E. Toop

slightly fresher. Even in a goods brake van with the doors closed, smoke seeped in, floated around and was quite visible to those present. On 20 November 1929 disaster struck.

Somerset & Dorset 2–8–0 freight locomotive No. 89, resplendent in her black livery, was working the 11.30 a.m. from Templecombe, due Bath at 6.15 p.m. As she toiled up the gradient of 1 in 100 from Midford towards Combe Down Tunnel, Driver Henry Jennings must have wondered how he would fare in the confines of the longest unventilated single-bore tunnel in Britain, for behind him he had a brake van and thirty-seven wagons, thirty-two of which were loaded with coal. One thing in his favour was that he was going tender-first as the Somerset & Dorset turntables were too short to turn this class of engine. This meant that the chimney was behind him and fumes were less likely to be a problem, unless there was a following wind to blow them forward. Soon after entering the tunnel, which was exceptionally hot and smoky, Fireman Maurice

Class 8F 2–8–0 No. 48444 emerges from the Midford end of Combe Down Tunnel. No. 48444 was built at Swindon in June 1944.

c. February 1966 C. Steane

No. 89 brand new at Bath MPD. Sheerlegs for lifting engines can be seen above the cab roof.

August 1925 Courtesy *Bath Chronicle*

The view from Combe Down Tunnel into Lyncombe Vale.

April 1966 C. Steane

Pearce of Midsomer Norton, was forced by the choking fumes to wrap a coat round his head and sit down, after which he remembered nothing, the poisonous gases having rendered him unconscious.

No. 89 was steaming badly, but Driver Jennings gallantly stuck to his post at the regulator until he too was overcome by fumes and fell into unconsciousness. The engine, now with two incapacitated men on her footplate, plodded on her laborious way up through the tunnel, the other side of which was a gradient of 1 in 50 down to Bath. Through Lyncombe Vale No. 89 picked up speed on the falling gradient helped by the weight of the thirty-eight vehicles behind her, plunged into Devonshire Tunnel and out the other side. Guard Christopher Wagner had applied the handbrake in his van, but without the help of the locomotive and tender brakes it was hardly more than a token gesture.

The train sped round the curve before Bath Junction and at a speed probably in excess of 50 mph crashed at the entrance to Bath goods yard, the wagons piling up in a great heap. The office cabin was demolished, killing Inspector John Norman, in charge of the yard, who was inside. One curious outcome was that a pencil on the office table was

The debris of crashed wagons at Bath. A Clandown colliery wagon is at the base of the pile, with one from Writhlington above.

20.11.29 Courtesy *Bath Chronicle*

A photograph taken at night of 2–8–0 No. 89 lying on its side having partly demolished the office cabin.

20.11.29 Courtesy *Bath Chronicle*

No. 89 as BR No. 53809 71G (Bath Green Park), leaving Norton Hill Colliery with a Down train.
15.4.55 Revd Alan Newman

driven into a sleeper for about half its length. Jack Loader, a young LMS clerk from Gloucester who was unfortunately taking a short cut through the yard on his way home from work, was killed when struck on the head by part of a gas lamp standard.

Railwaymen quickly arrived on the scene and extricated the footplate crew from the debris, laying them on wooden benches. Both were thickly covered with coal dust. Driver Jennings was found to be dead, but his fireman was alive, although badly injured; Guard Wagner was also hurt. Anticipating a pile-up at Bath Junction, he jumped from his van and on landing broke both kneecaps. Ironically, had he stayed in his van, he would have been unharmed, for after the crash the van still stood upright with his oil lamp burning brightly at the base of the handbrake column. If a guard has his brake on hard, and in this case Guard Wagner had it on very tightly, a van stops before hitting the buffers of the wagons in front of it. This led to another curiosity – a bottle of milk was found still upright on the table in the guard's van.

And what happened to No. 89? She was repaired and returned to service and continued to work over the Somerset & Dorset until her withdrawal in June 1964, and is now preserved at the Midland Railway Centre, Butterley. To avoid another footplate crew being overcome by fumes, S&D engines were given Welsh coal. Coal from the Bedwas colliery was considered the best – it made very little clinker so that at the end of a trip the fireman just raked the bars and the dust fell into the ashpan. Apart from giving off less fumes, Welsh coal withstood an engine pounding up gradients better than North coal did and a smaller quantity was used.

If a fireman had coal from places such as Radstock or Bristol, which clinkered badly, a bin of limestone was provided for laying on the fire bars. A fireman had two choices: he could either break up a large lump of limestone prior to putting it into the firebox, or place it in a large lump and let the heat from the fire crack it up. An alternative was to use ballast if this was the right size. Whatever was used, it was essential to avoid clinker forming a solid mass because this would prevent the access of air necessary for good combustion. Saltley men used old brick fire arches as a base for the fire. Radstock banking engines using Radstock coal required limestone all the time and their fires had to be cleaned after every other trip to Masbury.

North coal burnt more rapidly and frequent firing was worse at night for a driver because opening the firehole door, and thus allowing the brilliant light to come out, temporarily spoilt his night vision. If Bath ran short of coal, Bristol motive power depot sometimes sent over some North coal – one fireman said it 'burnt like paper'. Occasionally during the Second World War household coal had to be used and this burnt so quickly that 'it was like feeding donkeys with strawberries'. When Fred Epps fired with household coal he found it better to reduce the quantity of air to the fire by leaving the bottom firehole door up and firing over the top.

One day John Stamp was firing to Archie Gazzard on a Bath to Bristol St Philip's passenger train. John had not been on the job long and Archie said to him, 'We go to Barrow Road with three coaches and if we've got time, we'll go into the loco depot and stack up with North coal.' John believed North coal was superior to Welsh coal because all you had to do was to fill the firebox with as much as you could get in and it would burn easily, whereas Welsh coal required different and more careful treatment. At Barrow Road they placed the Johnson Class 1P 0–4–4T under the coal hopper and completely filled the bunker and also shovelled more into the fire box. They coupled to the train, backed down to St Philip's station and worked the train to Mangotsfield. Who should be on the platform there but Harry Whitaker, district locomotive superintendent for the Bristol, Gloucester, Bath and S&D area and son of Alfred Whitaker, the former S&D locomotive superintendent.

As they drew to a halt at Mangotsfield station, some lumps of coal, which unbeknown to the crew were on the cab roof, slid off with a crash right at Mr Whitaker's feet. He approached with his stick. 'What's this? Oh, it's you again Gazzard. I might have known it would be you. Fireman, are you responsible for this?' John asked, 'For what, Mr Whitaker?' 'This coal down here. Did you put it there?' John replied, 'It fell off the roof.' 'Fell off the roof!', he exclaimed, 'What do you mean, "Fell off the roof"?' Then Archie explained that they had been to Bristol MPD and filled the bunker so that they would not have to go to Bath shed for coal when they returned. Whitaker said, 'You

Class 1P 0–4–4T No. 1388 at Bristol St Philip's with a stopping train to Bath.

c. 1932 S. Miles Davey

must be more careful, that could have fallen on my head and done me an injury you know. I'm not entirely satisfied that you can do this job properly.' Mr Whitaker climbed into the cab and Archie said, 'Oh, I shouldn't come up here Mr Whitaker, we haven't got a pet pipe and it's very dirty!' 'Oh, never mind, Gazzard,' he replied, 'I'll risk that.'

The train set off and when they reached Warmley the engine started priming, so Archie had to open the cylinder cocks and all the way to Bitton steam and water blew out from underneath the engine. Whitaker remarked, 'Oh Gazzard, you've got the cylinder cocks open. Anything wrong?' 'Oh,' said Archie, 'I thought I'd better warm the cylinders Mr Whitaker, before we give them full pressure, there's some water in them.' 'Yes, Gazzard,' he said, 'I think you're doing the right thing. Carry on'. When they arrived at Bath Mr Whitaker said, as if he did not know, 'I want your names as I'll refer this to Mr White' – Tom White being the chief foreman at Bath – 'Don't let me see coal stacked like that on the roof again, or else it might be serious for you.'

Some owners of property adjoining a railway devised various ruses to obtain a free coal supply. One man living in the suburbs of Bath set up bottles on sticks at the bottom of his garden. The temptation was too much for most locomotive crews who threw coal at them to try and break them. Perhaps even less honest was a driver on the 8.15 p.m. passenger train from Bath to Bournemouth. As there were no passengers on his train between Evercreech Junction and Cole, he stopped near a farm and exchanged some coal for eggs. At Bristol, Barrow Road shed, coal wagons were moved

Class 1P 0–4–4T No. 1328 at Mangotsfield with a Bristol St Philip's to Bath stopping train.

c. 1925 S. Miles Davey

to the coaling tower by means of a capstan. One wagon was not checked and instead of being full of coal, was carrying pipes. These were tipped into the tower's hopper and it was a long and laborious task sorting the broken pipes from the coal in the storage bunker.

When a fresh fire was lit in an engine it gave off a considerable amount of smoke as combustion was imperfect. A schoolmaster who lived near Branksome shed, Bournemouth, complained bitterly of the smoke produced while steam-raising, so in order to pacify him, the fire was built up with coke instead of coal. Different types of engine needed different firing methods. S&D 'Large 4–4–0s' went best with a haycock fire. One day Fireman Ted Smith was on No. 67 with Driver Bill Brooks working the 10.10 a.m. passenger from Bournemouth West to Bath. Inspector Wells boarded the engine and insisted that it be fired with coal in the corners. As the crew anticipated, by using this method No. 67 was reluctant to steam and so was nine or ten minutes late arriving at Bath. When the guard approached with a Lost Time Ticket, Driver Brooks unsuccessfully tried to make the inspector accept the ticket. Bill wrote in his report that the lost time was due to obeying Inspector Wells' instructions.

One cunning driver slanted his window so that it reflected the view of coal on his fireman's shovel. If he considered there to be too much he knocked it on the floor with his foot. If firing was correct, a driver could see smoke issuing from the chimney. If coal was put on and no smoke appeared, a driver would instruct his fireman to use the pricker to open the fire and allow air to come in to improve combustion. After firing, he was required to sweep and water the floor.

Fireman Fred Epps had a frightening experience on S&D Class 7F 2–8–0 No. 13808. It was towards the end of the Second World War and lighting restrictions had been sufficiently relaxed to allow a few lamps in the shunting yard at Bath. Driver Charlie

BR Standard Class 4MT 2–6–0 No. 76065 heading the 1.10 p.m. Bournemouth West to Bath, near Cole and crossing the ex-GWR Reading to Taunton line.

28.10.61 Author

4–6–0 No. 7925 *Westol Hall* passes Bristol, Barrow Road MPD with a summer Saturday train to the West of England. A BR Standard Class 2–10–0 stands left, under the ash plant, while on the right can be seen part of the coaling tower.

24.7.65 E.T. Gill/Revd Brian Arman

Knight and Fred booked on at 10.00 p.m., then from the shed collected their engine which had been prepared by another set of men and backed it on to the goods train. That night the 10.20 p.m. to Bournemouth had a full load and the bank engine was back near Bath station signal-box. Fred pushed the tablet catcher out ready to collect the tablet at Bath Junction and began to be busily engaged in breaking up large lumps of North coal. Charlie opened the regulator and Fred felt No. 13808 violently rocking and rolling. He looked round to see what was wrong and saw he was alone on the footplate. Charlie had been flung out. The engine heeled over and Fred was left hanging out of the side, luckily unhurt. Fortunately two wheel flanges became caught in a check rail and prevented the engine turning completely over.

The cause of the accident was a steel plate approximately 3 ft by 2 ft, lying across the surface of a rail and made the pony truck derail. Normally a nearby gaslight would

No. 69, a sister engine to No. 67.

c. 1925 Author's collection

have illuminated the obstruction, but for some reason it was out that night. It was believed that the steel plate had fallen from a wagon of scrap metal. A steam crane was summoned from Gloucester and No. 13808 cut from its tender, eight hours having elapsed before she was righted. This mishap would have been less serious if the train had not been banked, for the banker, not knowing of the trouble at the front of the train, kept pushing until No. 13808's right-hand buffer was actually in the ground.

A fireman had to be careful not to overfill a boiler or his engine would prime – that is, throw water from the chimney. It was possible to tell when an engine was likely to prime because the water in the gauge glass became discoloured, so, on receiving this warning, you ran with a lower water level. One Bath fireman, who must remain anonymous, helped his driver prepare another engine for a turn before preparing his own. The fireman turned on his injector and went across to complete a task on the other engine.

Bath MPD: left to right: BR Standard Class 5 4–6–0 No. 73052; Class 4F 0–6–0 No. 44661 and Class 7F 2–8–0 No. 53808. An ash wagon is on the far right.

11.6.54 Revd Alan Newman

His driver, going round oiling, unfortunately failed to notice that he had left it on. The fireman only realised the problem when they tried to go off shed. The engine went on hydraulics instead of steam. Black, sooty water poured from the chimney as they passed over Victoria Bridge Road on what was a beautiful summer day. The following morning Shedmaster Harold Morris told the driver he had received a letter of complaint from a lady who had been on her way to the park dressed in a light summer frock. She had been drenched by the sooty water and put in a claim for damages.

The fireman was responsible for collecting a tablet giving authority to proceed over a single line. One day Fred Epps was firing to Driver Bert Perry on a 4–4–0 Compound working the Birmingham New Street to Bath Parcels train. It went round 'The Ditch' between Barnt Green and Ashchurch rather than using the main line down the Lickey Incline. Often there was a young signalwoman at Redditch South and as the engine came off the double track on to the single line, she stood so close that it seemed the engine would strike her, but her judgement was accurate and she was never hurt as she handed over the tablet.

At one box south of Redditch the veranda of the signal-box came close to the line and as it was single track on each side of the station, Fred Epps had to both give up the tablet for the section they were leaving and receive a tablet for the section ahead. Fred crouched down with his knees jammed against the handrails for security as he held the tablet he was giving up in his right hand and was ready to receive the new one in his left. He handed over the tablet to the signalman, but unfortunately the signalman held on to the one Fred should have collected. The engine was going slowly, but if Driver Bert Perry had not grabbed him to keep him on board, he would have been dragged off.

At Bath Junction the fireman of an S&D banking engine had to collect the banking tablet and as it was heavy and therefore receiving it could be quite painful, it was the practice to make an armpad from cotton waste. At Bath Junction the Whitaker tablet exchanging apparatus could only be used for offering a tablet to the engine at the head of a train, not a banker at the rear.

The flooded Victoria Bridge Road, Bath. To allow sufficient headroom, the road was lowered when the bridge was built.

1875 Courtesy *Illustrated London News*

Harold Morris talks to Driver Harold Burford on Class 8F 2–8–0 No. 48309, one of only two steam-heat

fitted engines of this class.

4.4.65 Hugh Ballantyne

At Newton Meadows, west of Bath, Class 4P 4–4–0 Compound No. 41194 pilots Class 2 2–6–2T
No. 41243 working the 9.05 a.m. Bristol Temple Meads to Bath. The Compound was proceeding to Bath to
work an Up express.

28.8.54 Author

One day Fred Holmes was on Class 2P 4–4–0 No. 696 firing to Sammy Mitchell. The
tablet was placed in the Whitaker apparatus on the tender before they reached Midford
where the single line ended and double track began. They believed all was well, but later
on the journey were stopped at Evercreech Junction and asked for the Midford tablet.
They said that it had definitely left the catcher and must have been knocked astray. It was
never found.

On another occasion Fred was working the 10.25 a.m. Bath to Bournemouth West
passenger. Before Stalbridge he placed the tablet in the exchanger and while he was so
occupied, was unable to keep a lookout on his side of the engine. Unfortunately, some
hounds were on the line and were cut to pieces. There were eight links in that roster, so
eight weeks later they were back on the same turn. This time he saw the hunt and got

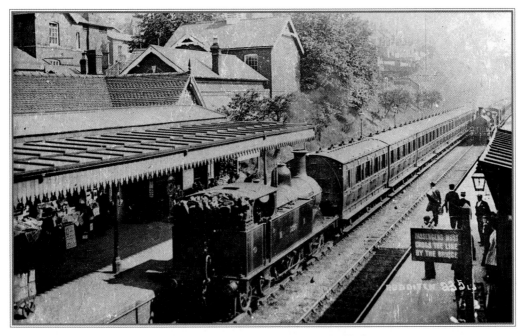

A Class 1P 0–4–4T with a stopping train at Redditch station.

c. 1910 Author's collection

Ashchurch station, view north. The Tewkesbury line curves left and the Redditch line bears right. An outside frame 0–6–0 with an Up goods stands on the Down line.

c. 1910 Author's collection

The Whitaker tablet exchanging apparatus. On the left-hand apparatus a pouch awaits collection, while on the right, the jaws are ready to snatch a pouch from the engine. Normally both are never swung out together; this view at Midford was only for photographic purposes.

December 1965 C. Steane

Class 2P 4–4–0 No. 40696 leaving Midsomer Norton with a Bath to Templecombe stopping train.

15.6.57 R.E. Toop

his driver to stop. The next day when they called at Blandford, a man came up and gave the driver an envelope which he put in his pocket without opening. A few days later the driver opened it and discovered it contained £5 – £3 for himself and £2 for Fred.

Len West was driving Class 2P 4–4–0 No. 696, the train engine of a double-headed Down troop special. It was night and at Midford he saw the tablet leave the catcher and gave a toot on the whistle to inform the driver of the leading engine that the exchange had been completed satisfactorily and that he could open his regulator. They were surprised to find adverse signals at Wellow and the signalman there said that his Midford colleague believed that the tablet had not been handed over. The crew of No. 696 explained that it had certainly left the engine. The ground around Midford signal-box was searched but to no avail and No. 696 was also thoroughly examined, including the ashes in the ashpan. About seven years later a leak occurred in the roof of the Hope & Anchor Inn at Midford. Builders went up to repair it and discovered the long-lost tablet.

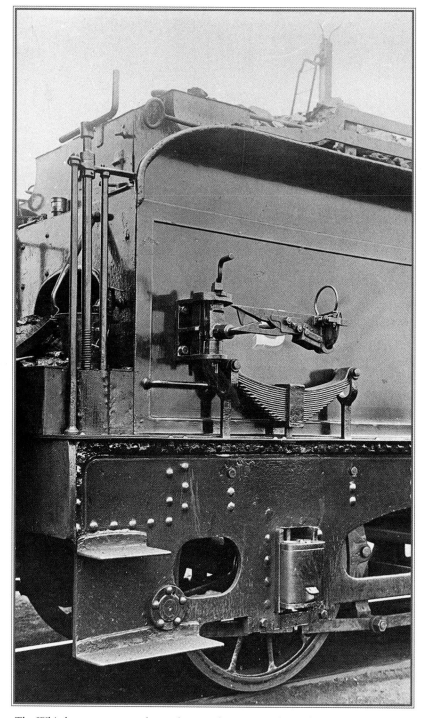

The Whitaker apparatus on the tender, seen here retracted into the travelling position. Behind the collecting jaws can be seen a pouch for collection. The tender is painted in S&DJR livery.

c. 1906 Author's collection

S&DJR 4–4–0 No. 71 heads a four-coach Down train at Stalbridge. Just 'S&D' on the buffer beam was unusual as the full initials were usually featured.

c. 1920 Author's collection

Fred Epps once saved a driver from causing what might have been a serious accident. He was returning from Birmingham on a 600 Class 2P 4–4–0 working the duplicate 'Pines Express'. Normally, a driver closed the regulator between Churchdown and Engine Shed Junction, Gloucester, but on this occasion he left it untouched. After passing the loco depot less than a mile from the station, Fred spoke reminding him of the station's proximity. They were still going at 60 mph at Tramway Junction and 40 mph as they reached the platform situated on quite a severe curve. Fred saw the footplate gradually edging towards the platform, but fortunately it did not strike. An off-duty driver standing on the platform was so scared 'that his hair stood on end'.

The signalman at Barton Street Junction signal-box a hundred yards or so beyond the platform had the foresight to open the gates and the train drew to a halt just beyond, before setting back to the platform. No one reported the matter so no more was said. The driver admitted to Fred that he had lost his bearings and if the fireman had not spoken he would have continued at speed and overturned. To obviate such a disaster, drivers were required to sign route cards every six months. If you knew a road one way,

Class 3P 4–4–0 No. 40745 passes Tramway Junction signal-box *en route* to Gloucester MPD.

July 1948 M.E.J. Deane

Gloucester, view Up. 1853 Class 4–2–2, probably No. 94, is seen on the right.

c. 1905 Author's collection

The Down 'Devonian' leaves Gloucester Eastgate behind 'Jubilee' Class 4–6–0 No. 45725 *Repulse*. Notice the elevated Barton Street Junction signal-box and the setting sun behind it to the right.

14.12.60 S.P. Derek

it did not necessarily follow that you knew it in the opposite direction because different skills were involved in going up a gradient to descending one.

Another instance of a driver not knowing better than his fireman occurred when Fred Holmes was on a Class 2P 4–4–0, probably No. 553, lent to Bath by Bristol Motive Power Depot for working the 'Pines Express'. Having had trouble with this engine the previous day, Bert Shipp advised Fred to 'Keep a good fire in it.' Less than a mile from Bath, before they passed through Weston station, Bert crossed over to Fred's side, took the fire iron down and levelled the fire off. He was not as successful at firing as Fred had been the day before and they were short of steam by the time they reached Tuffley Junction on the outskirts of Gloucester. They had No. 553 again the next day and Fred wondered whether the trouble lay with the exhaust steam injector being too fierce, so asked whether he could use the live steam injector on the driver's side. Receiving the authorisation to do this, he operated the live injector and steaming improved noticeably.

The attitude of a driver could make life pleasant or unpleasant for a fireman. Some drivers were friendly and helpful, willing, like Bert Shipp, to take the shovel if things went wrong, or to let their fireman have a turn at driving. Other drivers were morose and literally drew a line down the centre of the cab saying, 'That's my half, and that's yours. I don't want to see you crossing that line.' After making that statement they might

Class 2P 4–4–0 No. 40564 and 'West Country' Class Pacific No. 34043 *Combe Martin* head the Down 'Pines Express' at Midford.

5.8.61 Author

be silent for the rest of the trip. One driver at Stoke-on-Trent was sarcastic, but corrected gently: if a window on the fireman's side was dirty he would remark, 'You can look through my window if you can't see out of yours.' A driver might have more influence over a fireman than his parents, for he was in the driver's company for more waking hours. If a driver swore, gambled and drank to excess, then it was likely that his fireman would behave in a similar way.

Drivers could create difficulties for their firemen. Driver Edgar Gray used coal efficiently and approaching Midford with an Up goods train, as soon as he observed that the distant signal was 'off', opened his regulator and got up speed to rush the bank. Another driver was in the habit of passing through Midford very slowly which meant that the engine had to work hard up the bank and with this style of driving the fireman needed to fill the firebox at Midford. However, a fireman could also make life difficult for a driver. During the latter years of the S&D, in the summer when staff was short, a

A 2–4–0 heads a Down express past Tuffley Junction, the MR trailing left and the GWR right.

c. 1910 Author's collection

driver might have been given a junior fireman who was so inexperienced, or so weak, that he was not really capable of doing his job. This meant that sometimes on the return journey a driver might have had to fire as well as drive.

Footplate crews were very sectarian and at The Windmill public house (often nicknamed 'The Grinder' by enginemen) in Gloucester, GWR men would meet in one bar and the LMS men in another. At Bristol, LMS men sat on one side of a bar and those employed by the GWR on the other. Midland men talked of 'mashing' tea, whereas their GWR counterparts referred to 'brewing' or 'making' tea. The most successful footplate crews worked as a team. On one occasion Fireman Jack Barber was running 'light engine' from Westerleigh Marshalling Yard to Barrow Road MPD, Bristol. They had too large a fire in the box and his driver said, 'We'll have to get rid of it.' So saying, he opened the regulator wide and applied the tender hand brake. Lots of fire shot through the chimney and rattled back on the engine as at that time they were passing through Staple Hill Tunnel. This frightened the guard who had, until then, been enjoying his first footplate ride. However, they succeeded in ejecting most of the fire.

The 9.15 p.m. freight from Bath was a job for a senior driver as it commanded mileage money as well as the night rate. Crews arrived at Birmingham at about 5.30 a.m. and booked off. The railwaymen's hostel was situated by the gas works at Saltley – an unpleasant position because it meant you inhaled gas fumes while you slept. The law required railwaymen to book into a bed for eight hours. Two options were available and

A view from Midford station over the viaduct towards Radstock. Notice the 'x'-shaped backing signal authorising a movement from the single line to the Up road.

December 1965 C. Steane

The view towards Gloucester at the Westerleigh Marshalling Yard.

21.4.60 Author

the driver decided which was selected: go for a walk around the town, have lunch and go to bed; or go to bed on arrival and then patronise a cinema or theatre and then return to bed again for a few hours. You booked on at 12.30 a.m. the following day and worked the 2.10 a.m. Water Orton to Bath, arriving at Bath just before 8.30 a.m. This train mostly carried beer from Burton, or gas coal for Stapleton Road, Bristol, or for Bath gas works. The latter works used about fifty trucks of coal daily, some from Writhlington Colliery, Radstock, and some from the Midlands.

Although Regulations stated that railwaymen had to have twelve hours of rest between duties, this rule was ignored at Bath. One day when Colonel Harold Rudgard, Divisional Superintendent of Operation, Derby, was on a visit he was asked if this was satisfactory and replied, 'The Rule Book is made for fools, not men.' When footplate crews were working at night they always took the opportunity to have a nap if that was possible. A goods train held in a loop for other trains to pass might well remain stationary for a considerable time. To ensure that they would wake when the signal was pulled off for

Class 4F 0–6–0 No. 44263 emerges from Staple Hill Tunnel into the station.

21.4.60 Author

Saltley station, an unpleasant situation.

1968 D. Payne

Class 3F 0–6–0 No. 43507 held in a loop north of Charfield station to allow the 7.35 a.m. Nottingham to Bristol Temple Meads, headed by Class 5 4–6–0 No. 73031, to pass.

11.5.61 Author

them to proceed, a fireman hung a water bucket on the signal arm so that when the arm fell to indicate 'Clear', the bucket clattered to the ground and roused them. If standing head to tail with another goods train, a detonator was placed before a wheel of the brake van in front of their engine, so that when the preceding train moved forward, they were woken by the explosion and could move their train forward to take its place.

When disposing of an engine, most Bath drivers slaked down the ash and raked it out of the ashpan for their fireman, who was up above breaking clinker in the firebox and knocking down the fire. The fireman removed the remains of the fire – which had been allowed to die down as much as possible – from the centre of the firebox. Then, with the aid of a clinker bar, broke the clinker and exposed the fire bars, which had two hooks on the end. At Bath it was customary to lift the fire bars to facilitate fire dropping, but at Bristol and other sheds this practice was frowned upon. Three or four bars were removed, the number depending on how dirty the fire was. If the engine had been out for two days and the depth of clinker was quite severe, then four bars were taken out, but if it had only been on a short run, then just three bars were removed. The rear of the firebox was cleaned with a 'bent bar' and if the engine was wanted for further duties, a shovel or rake was used to push the fire forward, remove the clinker from the fire bars at the back, then pull the fire back and clean the front of the box. It was a strange thing that fire rested on top of clinker and it was quite an easy task to pull clean fire off clinker at the back of the firebox. The fireman then added a little more coal to keep it burning. Using a shovel, or rake, the remainder of the firebox contents were put down into the ashpan.

On modern engines equipped with rocking grate, fire cleaning was cleaner and easier. You simply opened the hopper doors under the engine and using an operating handle situated in the cab, shook the fire bars backwards and forwards. The hinged bars actually tipped up almost vertically. It was essential to ensure that no clinker jammed between the bars, otherwise they would have failed to return to the level position and would be damaged before the clinker cracked. The solution was to go underneath the engine with a long length of steel rodding and poke out the offending bits. A two-way stop and docking plate enabled the grate to be operated with a limited amount of movement so as to break up the clinker when running, or rocked fully to enable the fire to be dropped at disposal.

During the Second World War a Class 3F 0–6–0T was at work at Bath banking and shunting for twenty-four hours. It went to the shed at 2.30 p.m. for the fire to be cleaned and had been known to have most of the grate covered with clinker. Sometimes brickettes weighing 12 lb each were used during the Second World War and they made little clinker, but were very dirty and created a fine, grey ash, the quantity of which occasionally almost reached the brick arch. Pressure of work shunting and banking was such that the fireman had no time to improve his fire. When traffic eased in the postwar period, the banker/shunter went to the depot at about midnight so that some attention could be given to the fire. It was then in good condition to bank 'The Mail' and carry out other duties until it made a further visit to the shed at 2.30 p.m.

The afternoon shunting men booked on at 4.00 p.m. and the shunting inspector was waiting for them at the Boat Road – so named because it served a riverside wharf, where in previous years goods were transshipped between the railway and Midland Railway barges that plied along the Kennet & Avon Canal. The 0–6–0T's first duty was to place empty wagons into the siding of Stothert & Pitt, engineers, and draw out loaded vehicles, sometimes as many as fifteen bogies.

The 12.10 a.m. 'Ghost Train' from Bath was the heaviest of the day over the S&D and took Avonmouth traffic, which was all heavy, to Templecombe. When working an unfitted train, the vacuum ejector was shut down, the vacuum brake hooked up and the straight steam brake used. When John Stamp was firing a Class 8F 2–8–0 heading the 12.10 a.m., on several occasions going over the summit at Masbury the driver had applied the steam brake and John wound the tender handbrake on as hard as he could. However, the train still ran away out of control down the 8 miles or so, mostly at a gradient of 1 in 50, through Shepton Mallet, Evercreech New and Evercreech Junction. If you were running out of control, the practice was to sound a long whistle when passing the Evercreech Junction North distant signal to warn the Evercreech Junction

Wagons stand on the Boat Road. Beyond, on the left, can be seen the rear of the Bath MR locomotive shed, the stone base of the water tower (centre) and the S&DJR shed, right.

April 1966 C. Steane

South signalman to open the level crossing gates beyond the station. The 12.10 a.m. usually stopped at Evercreech Junction to pick up or put off wagons and often the crew used that opportunity to fill the water tank. If a train overran, the signalman called it back with a white or green lamp.

On one occasion on the 12.10 a.m., John had braking assistance from Binegar to Evercreech Junction. The banker had assisted the Up Mail from Evercreech Junction to Binegar and was waiting to return light engine. The 12.10 a.m. had Driver Alf Bolwell and ex-S&D Class 7F 2–8–0 No. 13803 and forty-six wagons of what was supposed to be goods but was mostly heavy stuff from Avonmouth, which should have been classified as mineral. In the 3¾ miles from Radstock to Chilcompton fifteen minutes were lost and at Binegar, Driver Bolwell seized the opportunity to use the banker to give braking assistance. It was coupled in front of No. 13803 and the vacuum brake hoses connected.

Class 7F 2–8–0 No. 53803 climbs the 1 in 157 gradient under the East Somerset Railway south of Shepton Mallet station.

22.8.57 Author

At Masbury Summit, 811 ft above sea level, the regulators of both engines were closed, the handbrakes applied and the driver on the front engine put the vacuum brake fully on. Driver Bolwell and Fireman Stamp were aware that the driver of the leading engine had fully applied the vacuum brake because they both saw the gauge on the train engine drop to zero. Nevertheless, that train, with two engines, ran away down over the Mendips and did not stop until it was a ¼ mile south of Evercreech Junction station. The brake van was alight owing to fire coming from its brake blocks and igniting the floor. It is said that when a van's brakes are on hard, if pulled by the engine the wheels revolve, but when the engine stops pulling, the wheels skid. The brake blocks of No. 13803 were worn to such an extent on that occasion that before it

Class 7F 2–8–0 No. 13800, having past beneath the GWR's Yatton to Witham line, enters Cannard's Grave Cutting with a coal train.

c. 1938 Author's collection

could return to Bath it had to go to the engine shed at Templecombe Lower to have new blocks fitted.

Early in the Second World War, Driver George Prentice and Fireman Fred Epps with a Class 7F 2–8–0 took a train carrying rolls of barbed wire on the 7.50 p.m. from Bath. The guard came up to the engine before they left Bath and reported a full load to George and Fred, though later they found that it well exceeded a full load. They struggled up to Masbury and descended carefully to Shepton Mallet, the brakes only just holding the train. At Cannard's Grave Cutting just beyond Shepton they crept over the summit and when they passed through the first arch beyond, George said, 'That's it, she's gone. Sit down, there's nothing you can do.'

Flames poured from the cast-iron brake blocks and 'You could see cows grazing in fields 200–300 yards away.' The young Fred Epps found the experience thrilling and was quite unafraid. They rushed through Evercreech New at 50–60 mph, the whistle wide

Evercreech New station, view Up.

c. 1965 C. Steane

open. The signalman rang Evercreech Junction and the branch train shunting there was quickly given refuge in a siding to give the runaway a through road. George Prentice drew his train to a halt a mile or so beyond Evercreech Junction, the engine's brake blocks completely worn away. As it would have been foolhardy to continue, they pushed the train back to Evercreech Junction and ran on 'light' to Templecombe to get a new set of brake blocks fitted.

The 7Fs had five brake cylinders: four on the engine for braking the driving wheels (the cylinder for the leading pair of driving wheels also worked the brake on the pony truck in early years), and one brake cylinder on the tender. In the days when cast-iron brake blocks were used, fragments from heated blocks were thrown into the motion, but the substitution of Ferodo blocks cured this trouble. At Saltley shed a cast-iron brake block lasted six months, whereas over the S&D it only gave one or two return trips between Bath to Evercreech Junction. Normally on the S&D, wagon brakes were not pinned down at the head of a gradient as this practice took too much time. John Stamp

LMS INTERNAL CORRESPONDENCE

Our Reference HD/E/50/4. Your Reference

1.11.43.

From OFFICE OF DIVISIONAL SUPERINTENDENT OF OPERATION.

BRISTOL 3. NOV 1943 MOTIVE POWER SECTION

DERBY

(Centre No. 49).

EXPT. D/LD.1216 Ferodo Brake Blocks.
Engine 13801, Bath.   19

     I attach E.R.O. 14017 relating to the above, together with Drawing D.16543, showing the special Ferodo Brake Blocks and details of clamping plates, etc. by which these blocks are attached to the permanent shoe. The object of the trial is to try to obviate rapid wear of slide bars due, it's suspected, to dust from the standard type of cast iron shoe normally used.

     In the case of wear, the Ferodo blocks only should be renewed and not the complete brake shoe (as detailed on the E.R.O. 14017).

     Instructions have been given for 4 renewal blocks to be despatched to Bath.

     It is not anticipated that any trouble will occur, or that the rate of wear will be so rapid as in the case of cast iron, but advice should be sent to the

pto.

C.M.E., London Road Offices, Derby, Ref. KH.5.T9/5, a copy of the advice to be sent to me, as soon as it is necessary to carry out any major adjustment or renewal of the blocks in order that a C.M.E. representative may be sent down to Bath to make observations.

     In the event of the results not being entirely satisfactory a representative of Messrs. Ferodo will also attend.

     Mr. C.E.Weston is arranging to call and see you regarding the experiment, on Friday next, 5th November.

for J.W.Watkins,

Letter dated 1 November 1943 from J.W. Watkins, Divisional Superintendent of Operations, to A.H. Whitaker, District Locomotive Superintendent, Bristol, regarding the trial of Ferodo brake blocks on Class 7F 2–8–0 No. 13801.

said that he had been on the turntable at Evercreech Junction and watched trains coming down the bank and it was like a 'Brock's Benefit Night' with fire and flames pouring from the locomotive wheels and all the guard's van wheels and the brake blocks red hot. When on the footplate, the flames and brightness from the blocks and wheels were so great that when passing Evercreech New at night John had been able to read the time of the church clock: 'From the engine came sheets of flame and the driving wheels were like great Catherine wheels and blue flames were round the guard's van wheels . . . You could see the rabbits playing in the fields.' Some drivers misused the brakes because they enjoyed seeing fire come from them if they were applied fiercely at speed.

The S&D had only two classes of train: either a fully fitted passenger or parcels, or a freight train. For many years the management refused to allow fitted vehicles and the vacuum brake to be operated. When the Western Region took over in 1958 shunters at Bath were told to shunt vacuum-fitted vehicles next to the engine and couple up the vacuum hoses and from that time many trains were partly fitted in this way.

Class 7F 2–8–0 No. 53805 shunts coal wagons from Norton Hill colliery at Midsomer Norton station.

14.8.59 Author

The signal-box and waiting shelter on the Down platform, Radstock North.

c. 1966 C. Steane

Apart from the S&D gradients causing rapid wear of the cast-iron brake blocks on the Class 7F 2–8–0s, dust from the blocks caused wear on the outside slide bars, motion and cylinders. To try and obviate these problems, in November 1943 Ferodo brake blocks were tried on the leading coupled wheels of No. 13801. Later all its driving wheels were fitted with Ferodo blocks, which proved so successful that they were fitted to the whole class. Although three or four times more expensive than those of cast iron, they lasted approximately four weeks instead of just one day and also eliminated wear on the slide bars. Furthermore, because they were lighter they were easier to fit. At first the Ferodo blocks became red hot and locked the wheels thus causing flats, so that when the brakes were released the engine would go 'bump, bump, bump'. Eventually, Ferodo technicians devised a better composition. Drivers soon learned that with an engine fitted with Ferodo blocks the brakes should never be applied fully, or the wheels would 'pick up'. At least one driver dropped sand when descending steep gradients to guard against the wheels locking.

The secret of descending a steep gradient safely with a goods train was to go slowly. If a train started running out of control, a driver was tempted to apply the brakes too fiercely causing the wheels to lock. This meant that he had to release the brakes, let the wheels turn and then re-apply the brakes and while this was happening the train was gaining more speed.

Driver Reg Beasley was on a coal train and experienced a narrow escape from disaster. He passed through Midsomer Norton and found the distant signal for Radstock was 'off'. Passing through Radstock station Guard Frank Staddon looked out and saw a man on the platform jumping up and down and yelling 'Stop the train!' Frank picked up his brake stick and wound the brake on hard. Fortunately no buffers locked, which tends to happen when the brakes are severely applied. At the far end of the platform Frank noticed a man with a red flag. When the train drew to a halt they could see that only about 20 yds beyond the engine a rail had been removed and the permanent way men had failed to inform the signalman of this fact. The locomotive crew did not make an official complaint as this would have cost the permanent way men their jobs.

A Down train approaches the derelict Winsor Hill signal-box and tunnel. Hamwood Quarry sidings are on the far right.

c. 1966 C. Steane

On one occasion when Frank Staddon was guard of an empty train from Templecombe he waved his lamp, but the engine driver made no attempt to open the regulator. The platform inspector addressed Frank, 'Guard, the driver will never start by your doing that.' 'Why not?' inquired Frank. 'Because your lamp is out,' was the reply. On investigation Frank discovered that some wet cotton waste had been thrust down the lamp's chimney and a lack of oxygen had extinguished the flame. Frank knew that Guard Archer was responsible and planned revenge. A box of sprats was consigned from Templecombe to Chilcompton for Downside School and two fish tails were protruding. These Frank cut off and wrapped round the inside of Archer's hand lamp. When Guard Archer lit it inside the shunters' cabin at Westerleigh Yard, other men there complained bitterly about the smell, believing it to be the fish oil in his lamp. He emptied and refilled it but it still stank. Eventually the sprats' tails were discovered.

One Up goods train shunted at Midsomer Norton and on completion of the station work, the shunter failed to couple up securely so that when the train left, the brake van and last ten wagons were left behind. As it was a down gradient to the next station, the quick-thinking guard released his brake and followed the train to Radstock, where the signalman was just closing the level crossing gates and then had to open them again rapidly.

At about 4.00 a.m. one summer's morning, Guard Dennis Macarthy was passing through Winsor Hill Tunnel on the Down line when the driver applied his brake to make sure he could check the train. When the driver released it, a coupling snatched and snapped. Dennis found that he had only about four wagons on his van and decided to run by gravity to Shepton Mallet where the engine would stop for water. On being told what had happened, the fireman said that he thought the van's sidelights looked rather a long way off.

Class 2P 4–4–0 No. 40698 of 71G (Bath) stands in the centre road at Bath Green Park.

3.3.54 Revd Alan Newman

Class 2P 4–4–0 No. 40696 at Bath MPD. Coal-loading tubs can be seen in the foreground.

c. 1959 R.J. Cannon/Author's collection

Chapter Two

DRIVERS

Driving a steam engine was a highly responsible job. There were many things that could distract a driver's attention and very occasionally mishaps occurred. One driver tried to draw a goods train out of the sidings at Saltley, but failed as the train was really too heavy for his engine. He made several attempts, but then the signalman grew tired of waiting, threw the signals against him and let a salt train come out. The driver of the heavy goods managed to get his train moving, failed to see the adverse signals and felt a bump as a buffer punched a hole in the side of a salt wagon. There was no derailment and he reversed; no one seemed to have noticed the accident and nothing was ever said.

The company's Rule Book & Appendix controlled a driver's actions from the moment he signed on to the time he signed off. Before taking charge of his engine he obtained copies of notices affecting his particular route and signals, and any engineer's department or other work; details of lineside slips; the likelihood of huntsmen and hounds crossing the line; water supply notices and any special instructions regarding his train or any other train that could have a bearing on the running of his own train.

A driver would then check to see that any report regarding repairs or adjustment to his own engine had been attended to and before leaving the shed assure himself that the engine was in running order to carry out the work required of it. He had to have road knowledge to decide whether a load was suitable. A driver was also responsible for work done by his fireman and was expected to verify any signals his fireman transmitted to him. On a single line the driver had to confirm that the tablet, or key, was correct for that section. When his turn of duty ended he was required to report any incidents and whether 'Repairs' or 'No Repairs' were required on his locomotive. He put in a statement of work performed and then disposed of the engine unless previously relieved. Finally, he signed off duty.

Some drivers were lacking in self-confidence. Not all Somerset & Dorset men, for example, were happy to work from Bath to Birmingham because on the S&D they generally encountered single signals on posts and found an array on a large gantry quite frightening and bewildering. Harry Whitaker, District Locomotive Superintendent, asked one Bath driver why he did not sign for the Birmingham road. The driver replied in his funny, high voice, 'Mr Whitaker, the signals there are like stars in the sky.' Harry Whitaker was strict and would not allow his men to smoke on duty and if he saw them doing so, gave them a dressing down.

At Templecombe S&D trains used a platform on the opposite face of the Southern Railway's Up platform. This meant that all S&D trains calling had to reverse in or out because a passenger train, with the exception of push-and-pull units, was not allowed to reverse unless it had an engine on what then became the leading end. This ruling meant that a spare engine had to be available to take passenger trains either in or out of Templecombe station.

One day in about 1946 the 1.40 p.m. Bournemouth West to Bath drew up at Templecombe Junction ready for reversal into the platform. 'Righto, dummy's off,' called his fireman and Archie Gazzard opened the regulator of his engine which was to couple up to the rear and draw it into the platform. Unfortunately, Archie opened the regulator too much and he crashed into the 1.40 p.m. Quite a proportion of the coal in the tender

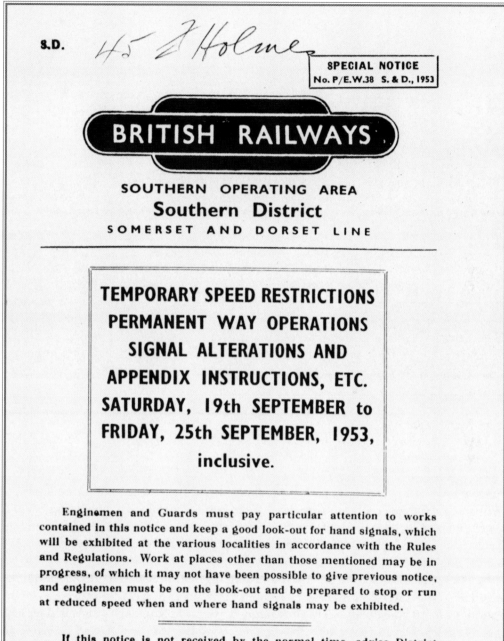

S.D. *45 F Holmes*

SPECIAL NOTICE
No. P/E.W.38 S. & D., 1953

BRITISH RAILWAYS

SOUTHERN OPERATING AREA
Southern District
SOMERSET AND DORSET LINE

TEMPORARY SPEED RESTRICTIONS
PERMANENT WAY OPERATIONS
SIGNAL ALTERATIONS AND
APPENDIX INSTRUCTIONS, ETC.
SATURDAY, 19th SEPTEMBER to
FRIDAY, 25th SEPTEMBER, 1953,
inclusive.

Enginemen and Guards must pay particular attention to works contained in this notice and keep a good look-out for hand signals, which will be exhibited at the various localities in accordance with the Rules and Regulations. Work at places other than those mentioned may be in progress, of which it may not have been possible to give previous notice, and enginemen must be on the look-out and be prepared to stop or run at reduced speed when and where hand signals may be exhibited.

If this notice is not received by the normal time, advise District Traffic Superintendent, Bath, by telephone.

S. W. SMART,
Superintendent of Operation.

B7½

Cover of Working Notices dated 19 to 25 September 1953. It was issued to Driver Fred Holmes.

A driver, oilcan in hand, stands on the running plate of S&DJR 4–4–0 No. 16.

c. 1910 Author's collection

rolled on to the footplate and, perhaps more seriously, their tea can fell to the floor and overturned. The parcels van on the rear of the passenger train was lifted a little and a buffer stem split. The men on the front engine were quite unaware of the mishap because the train's brakes were fully applied, but if they had been slack they would have felt the impact. They kept quiet about the incident and nothing was said.

Archie, a noted natural comic, enjoyed teasing his fireman. One day pounding up the gradient towards Masbury Summit he saw a crow on the line ahead and closed the regulator. 'What are you doing that for?' inquired Fireman Stan Shellard. Archie replied, 'I must stop. I can't run over that crow or I'll get bad luck for life!' Archie was quite an educated man and once wrote out a report in shorthand.

The fun was not all one-sided. At Mangotsfield the 6.30 a.m. passenger train from Bath went in the Down bay siding known as 'behind the box'. While waiting on his 600 Class 2P 4–4–0 Archie turned to light his pipe with the aid of a petrol lighter. Repeatedly the flint failed to produce a spark to light the wick. Frustrated, he hurled it through the tender doors right back into the coal. Using a spill made from a long length of paper, he successfully lit his pipe from the fire. Returning to Bath, his pipe went out and he was unable to use the spill method as the engine was in motion and the draught

Class 2 2–6–2T No. 41249 at Templecombe station with a Stephenson Locomotive Society special. Class 8F 2–8–0 No. 48706 and BR Standard Class 4 2–6–4T No. 80043 are at the other end of the train.

6.3.66 C. Steane

On the right, Class 8F 2–8–0 No. 48706 and BR Standard Class 4 2–6–4T No. 80043 haul at Stephenson Locomotive Society special into Templecombe station, while Class 2 2–6–2T No. 41249 waits on the left. Following this train's arrival at the platform, No. 41249 will move to what was the rear of the train to haul it out, before it proceeds southwards headed once more by No. 48706 and No. 80043.

6.3.66 C. Steane

A view of Mangotsfield station showing the line to Bath on the left; 'behind the box' siding right. The siding received this name because of its situation at the rear of the signal-box.

21.4.60 Author

drew the flames away from the firehole door. He asked his fireman if he had seen his lighter and received the reply, 'You've forgotten, you threw it back in the tender.' Archie assumed it had been shovelled on the fire with the coal and went for hours without his soothing smoke. Going off-duty the fireman produced the lighter from his pocket where he had put it after Archie threw it away.

On another occasion Len West was firing to Archie Gazzard on a trip to Birmingham. Preparing for their return, at a water crane they found the leather bag unusually wide and had to fold it in half to insert it into the tender. Unfortunately when the water was turned on the bag was forced out and soaked Archie who had to make the trip back to Bath in his longjohns and cap, the rest of his clothes hung up to dry in the cab.

One driver who was running round his train at Bristol St Philip's, failed to notice an open catch point and his engine went on the ground. Thinking quickly, he took the pressure gauge glass protector off, smashed the glass and claimed that the gauge glass broke, distracted his attention and that was the reason he went off the road. His excuse was not accepted and he lost two days' work.

Drivers did not always return home empty-handed. Sometimes they were able to obtain bean sticks from the lineside or produce purchased from farms or small holdings. One day when Driver Bob Ford drew into Warmley station with a Bath to St Philip's stopping train, on the platform a man with a dead fowl under his arm asked Bill if it was the train for Bristol. Bob said, 'Yes, why not travel on the footplate?' The man accepted the offer and in conversation it transpired that the man owned a poultry farm and was taking the dead bird for autopsy. A few days later the man thanked Bob for the footplate trip by giving him five sacks of hens' manure for his allotment. For the rest of his turn Bob carried the stinking ordure on the footplate and on arrival at Bath secured a porter's trolley to carry it on the remainder of the journey home.

A senior passed fireman was placed on the Bath shunter/banker link where he could be easily found if needed to work a longer distance train. Near Bath Junction signal-box was a pile of sawn-off sleeper ends left over following the completion of a newly laid turnout. Archie Gazzard lived in a house backing on to the line and, as he had left the railway by then, his old colleagues thought he would appreciate a couple of these offcuts. The plan was to drop them on their return from banking a goods train to Combe Down Tunnel. Approaching Archie's back garden, the driver slowed and the fireman kicked the offcuts from the footplate down the 20 ft high embankment and they travelled through

Class 2 2–6–2T No. 41240 leaving Bristol St Philip's.

c. 1950 Lens of Sutton

Class 7F 2–8–0 No. 53806 passes Warmley station with a coal train for Bath gas works.

28.4.62 R.E. Toop

the wire fence at its foot. Archie saw the fireman a few days later and told him that the sleeper ends had gone through the wall of his next door neighbour's fowl house and that he, Archie, had to repair it. (An interesting sequel was that when the author related this story to his father's cousin who lived in the same road, it transpired that the henhouse belonged to the author's great uncle.)

One driver was interested in fossils and when his engine was at Shepton Mallet an interesting large one was discovered in the coal. His fireman and guard helped him place the fossil on the front buffer beam and the driver tipped it off passing the brickyard south of Bath Junction. After going off-duty, the driver secured a pair of sack trucks and used them to carry his fossil home.

Fred Epps drove the longest ever fitted freight train from Poole to Templecombe. It consisted of twenty-six vans containing racing pigeons. Although close-coupled, there was still a certain amount of slack and he had to be careful to avoid snatches which could have broken the couplings. The Class 8F 2–8–0 had worked to Bournemouth and he ran

The 11.05 a.m. Bath to Evercreech Junction climbs the 1 in 50 out of Bath with Class 4F 0–6–0 No. 43995 as train engine, assisted in the rear by No. 44096 of the same class.

12.2.55 R.E. Toop

light engine from Bournemouth to Poole yard. It was the intention that he would take twenty vans, but the guard said 'The foreman wants to know if you'll take the rest.' Fred replied, 'How many?' 'Half a dozen'. 'Oh, all right, I'll do it to help out, but tell him he must get the signalman at Broadstone to let me have the distant off because I don't want to have to stop on the 1 in 75 bank.' The bargain was kept and Fred found the Broadstone distant signal off. Fred said that with a train of that length he felt a tug when the gradient changed.

Fred Epps recalled that one day he was driving a Class 5 4–6–0 with twelve coaches behind the tender when he stopped at Blandford for water. It was quite difficult stopping there as the gradient fell, was level and then rose. While the tender was being filled, Guard Jack Hopkins came up to the engine and said that a woman had complained that a case had fallen from the luggage rack when the train braked. From then on, to stop more smoothly, Fred used a trick he had learned from a driver while

Blandford Forum station, view Up.

4.5.63 Author

refreshing himself on the Gloucester to Birmingham road. Before applying the brake he opened the large ejector a little and, although not considered good practice, it certainly provided a smoother stop.

If an engine was steaming badly, a driver placed a 'jimmy' or 'chopper' on the blast pipe to divide the blast and so brighten the fire. A 'screw' was a similar device, but retained in place by a screw instead of a brake block. S&D Class 7Fs had a tool box on the front of their tenders and in it were two breakdown hooks, which drivers discovered could be placed in the blast pipe to sharpen the blast. The authorities frowned on these various practices but had crews not adopted them, many more trains would have had to stop for a 'blow-up'. A skilled ear could tell if an engine had been doctored with a 'jimmy', for when it was working hard it gave out a whistling sound. In the mid-1930s the Up 'Pines Express' from Bath was worked by a Birmingham crew and they used a 'jimmy' on the Class 2P 4–4–0s.

1282 Class 2–4–0 No. 157 and 890 Class No. 92 at Bath. No. 92 is being prepared to work the 2.00 p.m. non-stop Bath to Mangotsfield.

1934 Revd Alan Newman

Class 5 4–6–0 No. 45335 standing on a centre carriage road in Brunel's terminus, Bristol Temple Meads.

9.6.62 Author

Working over the Mendip Hills in winter could be most unpleasant, especially on engines with cabs that offered little shelter – one side of your body would be frozen by a cold draught and the other side roasted. Sometimes snow drifts would be encountered. George Allcock was firing to Driver Frank Hancock on an Evercreech Junction to Bath goods which became stuck in a snow drift in Masbury cutting. George Allcock started to walk forward to Binegar to alert the signalman there. Meanwhile, as the train was taking a long time to arrive, the Binegar signalman despatched a snow plough to search for it. It was very fortunate for George that he did so for they found him ensconced in a very deep drift with just his head protruding above the snow.

Some drivers had their own ways of making life easier for themselves. In the early 1930s some 2–4–0s were used on Bath to Bristol St Philip's stopping trains and an engine with this wheel arrangement was just short enough to be turned on the table at St Philip's. An engine had to be accurately balanced on the table or it was impossible to turn. Normally, Fireman Fred Holmes jumped down and shouted out when an engine was just about to go down indicating that the table was balanced, but on his first trip there with

Class 8F 2–8–0 No. 48706 works through Wellow tender-first with an Up goods.

c. 1965 C. Steane

Driver Bert Shipp, he was ordered to remain on the footplate. This was because Bert did everything by markers and knew it was balanced when it was alongside a certain mark.

Midland Railway engines had right-hand drive and if a water column was on the left side, Bert had a marker so that he knew exactly where to stop. Once he let Fred drive into Bristol Temple Meads, run round the coaches and then pick up water from the column. At this point Bert used a Craddock's shoe advertisement as a marker and told Fred, 'I'll tell you when to stop.' The coaches had to be positioned so that when the engine ran round and coupled on the other end, the tender was in the right place for the bag to go in. It was necessary for this procedure to be accurate within a few feet. However, when Bert called 'Stop!', Fred ignored him. Bert exclaimed sharply, 'You didn't stop where I told you!' Fred replied, 'You wait and see.' He ran the engine round the train and the engine was in exactly the right place for the bag to go into the tank. Puzzled, Bert said, 'I can't understand that.' He was unaware that Fred anticipated that the advertisement might be moved or removed and so had a mark of his own – a new railing post level with the driver when he stopped. Fred's foresight stood him in good stead.

This document details walking time allowed at Bath to various parts of railway property where train crews boarded or left their engines.

Apparently, some goods guards were not too intelligent or simply failed to allow for the varying weights of trains. On one lightly loaded train a guard quite unnecessarily applied his brake near Wellow. The driver purposely took no action, the train ground to a halt and he sent his fireman back to enquire why the guard had stopped the train. Some footplatemen were very resourceful, and cooked food on a shovel in the firebox. Goods guards had their own system for preparing food. They took an oily rag, wiped their stove shovel clean and cooked bacon and eggs on the stove in their brake van.

One driver never wore a watch and believed that had the railway company wished a driver to have one, they would have supplied it; he was only presented with one when he retired. He did all his driving by estimating the time. When driving a freight train he found that if you could count the sleeper ends going by, you were going too slowly and therefore losing time. One guard at Evercreech Junction boasted that his watch was both shockproof and waterproof. While Driver Attwell was inspecting it he cast it into the water tank saying, 'Well, let's test it then.' Unfortunately, he had to drain the tank to recover his timepiece.

Somerset & Dorset Joint Railway document showing the time allowed for the preparation and disposal of engines. This document was duplicated in the loco shed office, Bath, *c.* 1925.

Chapter Three

THE SECOND
WORLD WAR

The Somerset & Dorset Railway was a vital link providing a route from the Midlands to the south coast and was invaluable before the invasion of Normandy in 1944 carrying troops and their equipment. The S&D was also of use to the Germans. Although not corroborated by an enemy pilot, it was generally believed that German bombers heading for Bristol followed the S&D route northwards from the coast near Poole.

One beautiful summer's morning, Driver Ron Gray was on a Class 7F 2–8–0. He had worked the 3.30 a.m. Bath to Evercreech Junction goods and was returning with the 6.35 a.m. Evercreech Junction to Moorewood train of empty stone wagons. No air-raid warning was given at Shepton Mallet, but emerging from the 126-yd-long Winsor Hill Tunnel the engine was machine-gunned, bullets landing in the tender. Fortunately, Ron and his fireman were unhurt and able to continue to Moorewood to collect a stone train to take to Shepton where they were relieved and returned home 'on the cushions'. Winsor Hill Tunnel seemed a popular target for German planes as Oscar Pitt was also gunned by a Nazi fighter and stopped his train in the tunnel for shelter.

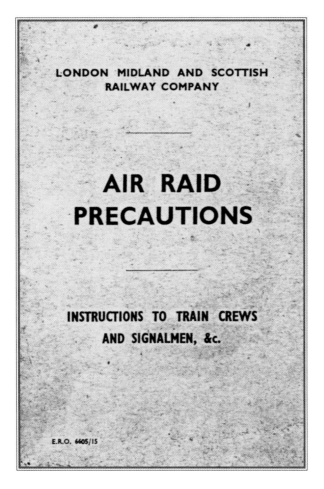

LONDON MIDLAND AND SCOTTISH RAILWAY COMPANY

AIR RAID PRECAUTIONS

INSTRUCTIONS TO TRAIN CREWS AND SIGNALMEN, &c.

E.R.O. 6605/15

Cover of an 'Air Raid Precautions' booklet issued to LMS staff in November 1938. Principal instruction covered how to cope with poisonous gas and the use of respirators. It also contained a small section on dealing with incendiary bombs.

The Up 'Pines Express' headed by Class 2P 4–4–0 No. 40563 and BR Standard Class 5 No. 73074 pass Moorewood sidings, which can be seen on the left.

25.6.55 R.E. Toop

One night when a German plane passed over Shepton Mallet signal-box travelling northwards, Venner, the signalman, rang Binegar and advised him to put his lights out as it had gone over so low that 'It nearly knocked my chimney pot off.' Ten minutes later the Binegar signalman, neither hearing or seeing any signs of the invader, believed that the warning was a joke and rang Venner to tell him so. Venner replied, 'No, it's true.' The next morning a German bomber was found upside down on Masbury Ring with five dead airmen inside.

On one occasion a Cole signalman, Sid Pitt, found all his instruments and bells for the section on one side of his box completely dead and wondered what had happened. While still pondering the reason for this, he heard someone mounting the signal-box steps. It was a man wearing RAF uniform who said that he had crashed and thought his

The view through the 126-yd-long Up bore of Winsor Hill Tunnel towards the signal-box.

31.7.59 Author

plane had cut the telephone wires. Sid said 'So it's you who's caused all this trouble!' and seemed more concerned with his bells and blocks than with the crashed airman. The pilot's colleague was later found suffering with a broken leg in a field.

A driver of Class 4F 0–6–0 No. 4557, an ex-S&D engine, carried a .303 rifle on the footplate as a means of defence. At Stalbridge a Spitfire, practising an attack for use on a German train, swooped down. The driver, believing he was being attacked by a German aircraft, shot two bullets into the Spitfire and wounded the pilot. Rifles were withdrawn from the footplate following this incident.

At the start of the Second World War gas attacks were expected and yellow gas-detecting paint was applied to a level of 6 in on the glass of a cab window. Footplate crews and guards were issued with service gas masks and black, steel helmets. This was a general issue to all and not just for those operating trains travelling through areas likely to be attacked. The helmets were only worn when an air raid was in progress and were essential because shrapnel could fall like rain. Fireman Archie Gunning recalled that on

Class 8F 2–8–0 No. 48706 and BR Standard Class 4 2–6–4T No. 80043 at Shepton Mallet station with a
Stephenson Locomotive Society special.

6.3.66 C. Steane

one occasion when he was in a Birmingham blitz his driver sheltered under the engine
but expected him to stay on the footplate and maintain the fire and water.

Early in the war Fred Epps was firing to Bill Leigh on Bournemouth West to Bath
passenger train. He recounts:

> We'd left Wincanton and were on the straight towards Shepton Montague. I suppose
> we'd got about ¾ mile away from Shepton Montague and we could see this plane
> down below the arch – there was a very high arch there. We saw him go up and then
> come down ever so low towards us. Bill and me didn't know what to do! We thought
> it was a Jerry. Eventually it went over the top and we could see it was one of ours . . .
> but it was a frightening experience.

Fred continued:

Class 4 4–6–0 No. 75071 approaches Cole station with the 1.10 p.m. Bath to Templecombe.
28.10.61 Author

One night we were coming back with the engine off the Down Mail with Driver Frank Hancock. We stopped at Blandford where we were given the Red Alert, so we immediately dropped the blackout sheets over the cab to hide the fire.

We pulled out of Blandford and going over the top was a park and then we started to go down to Stourpaine. Suddenly, out of the sky came the searchlight of a plane. It frightened us as we thought we were going to be bombed, or machine-gunned. Then we realised it was the landing light of a British plane!

'Alerts' were given verbally to train crews by signalmen who stopped trains for this purpose. A 'Yellow Alert' meant that raiders had crossed the coast, so the firebox doors were shut and blackout sheets erected. A 'Red Alert' indicated raiders were overhead, or in the close vicinity, so that if you had not already closed the firebox and erected the blackout sheets, you should do at once. If you were on a freight train descending a steep gradient – between Masbury and Evercreech Junction for example – a driver proceeded extremely slowly so that the cast-iron brake blocks did not glow and form a target for the enemy.

Because of the almost continuously varying gradients on the S&D, a guard was frequently applying, or releasing his brake particularly between Midford and Radstock. A sixty-wagon train could easily be on three different gradients at once and it was the guard's task to prevent the wagons from bumping into the engine. This was particularly awkward when a Red Alert had been announced and speed restricted to 15 mph because it was not as easy to keep the wagons 'off the engine' when moving at a slower speed. The guard's job was made more difficult when wagons with oil, rather than grease, axle boxes became common, as they ran more freely.

Class 4F 0–6–0 No. 4557 as S&DJR No. 57 near the weighbridge, Highbridge works. It received the No. 4557 in 1930 when the LMS took over the S&D locomotive stock.

c. 1925 Author's collection

Archie Gunning, left, with Locomotive Inspector Jack Dowell at Bath.

c. 1960 Author's collection

View Up at Wincanton station.

4.5.63 Author

Ted Smith experienced an air raid at Avonmouth. Incendiary bombs were dropped and he sheltered under the tender with his young fireman. Then, during a lull in the action they ran to an air-raid shelter. Already hiding there were two sets of GWR men who later went out and were killed. Following the raid, Ted and his fireman went to a pub, but the German raiders returned and so the railwaymen had to go back to the shelter. In this second raid a bomb destroyed a shunting engine and signal-box, the signalman fortunately being safe in a shelter. After the 'All Clear', Ted and his mate doused wagon fires with buckets of water.

Bert Perry and Fireman Fred Epps were on the Birmingham Parcels train that stopped at King's Norton for milk to be unloaded, unfortunately during an air raid. To speed up the unloading, Fred went back along the platform and assisted the Guard Reg Moore and a porter. All of a sudden the porter shouted, 'Get down quick!' Reg threw himself across the platform and hit his head and, even though he was wearing his steel helmet, he

Class 7F 2–8–0 No. 53808 passes through Staple Hill station with an Avonmouth to Bath freight.

c. 1955 Author's collection

View Up at King's Norton station.

c. 1910 Author's collection

Class 4F 0–6–0 No. 43886 arrives at Birmingham New Street with a train from Cromer.
5.7.58 Michael Mensing

was unconscious for a few moments. A bomb had fallen 300 to 400 yds behind the station. The train was undamaged and they proceeded, but their troubles were not yet over. While eating their food in the guards' room at Birmingham New Street station, bombs caused plaster to fall from the ceiling and that same night a railway fireman was killed at the station.

On another occasion Driver Alexander and Fireman Gray worked the 9.50 p.m. Bath to New Street Parcels. They booked on at 9.20 p.m. and set off on time. Because Birmingham was enduring an air raid their train was stopped at King's Norton, where they put on their 'tin hats' and sheltered under the tender. No trains ran in or out of New Street that day because, although it did not receive a direct hit, the signalling was damaged. Driver Alexander and Fireman Gray did not arrive back at Bath until 6.00 p.m. the following day.

Class 8F 2–8–0 No. 48706 and BR Standard Class 4 2–6–4T No. 80043 stand on the bridge over the River

Avon heading a Stephenson Locomotive Society special. Notice that it is on one of the centre roads.

6.3.66 C. Steane

A farm removal train at Bitton station. On the left can be seen the goods shed and sidings.

September 1933 Courtesy *Bath Chronicle*

A signalman at New Street was walking back to his box after filling his coal bucket when he looked up to watch a dog fight between British and German planes. This distraction caused him to trip over a rail and, while lying across the line, he became aware of a train almost upon him. There was no time to stand and move away – the only escape from death was to lie down between the rails. Unfortunately, his coat became caught under the train and he was dragged along until it stopped. He was so seriously injured that he was off work for a year and when he did at last return, could only carry out signalling duty at boxes with less intensive traffic.

During one air raid at New Street a fireman shovelled an incendiary bomb that fell on his footplate. Then, shortly after leaving the station and entering a tunnel, another incendiary bomb fell down a ventilating shaft and landed on the running plate. The driver stopped the train and the fireman clambered along the running plate and shovelled it off.

As the bombing of the river bridge just outside of Bath station would have marooned the two sets of coaches used on the S&D, each evening they were taken for storage at Bitton, now the headquarters of the Avon Valley Railway. While shunting these coaches in the blackout, a guard slipped and had his legs amputated. He lay there helpless, but as a qualified first-aider he instructed other railwaymen what they should do. After he had recovered and been fitted with artificial limbs, he operated the weighbridge at Bath.

During the Baedeker raids on Bath, 25 and 26 April 1942, the shed foreman had the foresight to disperse engines to various parts of the yard so that had a bomb fallen on the

Class 2P 4–4–0 No. 40696 at Bath with Stothert & Pitt's engineering works beyond. Notice the tablet catcher on the front of the tender and 'British Railways' and the early BR totem featured on the side.

September 1961 Revd Alan Newman

shed, the damage would have been minimised. In the event, no engines were hit directly, though blast from bombs blew out many signal lamps. For some days afterwards there was no lighting in the shed as the gas works had been so severely hit and an emergency lighting set was taken from the breakdown vans and installed in the shed.

Driver Frank Hancock, who had arrived with the last passenger train of the day and had been carrying out shunting duties at the station on Class 2P 4–4–0 No. 696, spent the whole of the blitz on the river bridge outside Bath station. He reported that some of the German planes were so low that if he had a bean stick he could have touched them. Incendiary bombs ignited the goods depot offices and a bomb dropped in Stothert & Pitt's works adjacent to the railway scattered sheet metal, girders, boulders and stone over the main line. Driver Harry Miles and Driver Walter Lake, who arrived at Bath down the S&D with two light engines after the first wave of bombing, were killed when the

Kirtley double-framed Class 1F 0–6–0 No. 2848 outside the former MR shed at Bath.

c. 1930 Author's collection

attackers returned a few hours later and the public shelter where they were taking cover on their way home received a direct hit.

Railwaymen had their own air-raid shelter below the stone-built ex-Midland Railway shed at Bath. As it would have disrupted railway services too much had railwaymen taken shelter every time an air-raid siren sounded, a plane spotter was positioned on top of the water softener and rang a bell when hostile aircraft were actually sighted approaching. On one occasion this spotter was shot at by a German plane.

LMS railwaymen made up a Home Guard platoon at Bath, and those who were not members were required to undertake fire-watching duty from the top of the goods shed. The Home Guard patrolled round the yard to ensure that German spies had not altered points to derail a train. One over-enthusiastic Home Guard shot at a railway guard who failed to identify himself when challenged in Bath goods yard, but fortunately the bullet missed.

Bath MPD with the water softener seen on the left and Class 2P 4–4–0s No. 40700 and No. 40569. The
S&DJR shed is in the centre and Class 7F 2–8–0 No. 53802 on the coaling stage road to the centre right.

28.3.59 Author

In 1941 a large gun travelled from the north of England to Portland. The GWR was
unable to create a path for it and it travelled via the LMS and S&D. As it was so long, it
was carried at each end on two bogies, the gun itself linking the pairs of bogies. Driver
George Prentice and Fireman John Stamp took it from Bath over the Mendips behind a
Class 7F 2–8–0, believed to be No. 13803. As they shunted it into Masbury sidings to
allow another train to pass, they heard shouts – its weight had spread the road.

A large petrol dump was installed at Masbury and a loop line laid to serve
underground and above ground storage tanks. Apparently shortly after Dunkirk when a
German invasion was expected, eight trains of petrol were run from Masbury to Poole
and had the invasion taken place, the petrol would have been floated on the water and
ignited. A United States' diesel locomotive shunted the United States Army sidings at
Masbury and on one occasion it was allowed to stray from the sidings and struck Class 2P
4–4–0 No. 499. The diesel fared worst, its US crew leaping off before it overturned.

The LMS Home Guard on the arrival platform, Bath.

c. 1941 Author's collection

The Midland goods shed at Bath after track lifting.

20.12.67 Author

Class 7F 2–8–0 No. 53803 climbing the gradient of 1 in 50 and about to pass under Claude Avenue bridge, Bath.

September 1952 Revd Alan Newman

Guard Frank Staddon was in charge of a train of eight Churchill tanks from Wool on the Bournemouth to Dorchester line, proceeding northwards to Bath behind a Class 7F 2–8–0 and Class 4F 0–6–0. At Evercreech Junction Frank asked for a banker, but the shunter there said, 'No, you can't have one because your train has two engines already.' Frank replied, 'I want a banker in case of a breakaway because my handbrake wouldn't hold that weight.' The shunter observed, 'Well, the wagons are vacuum fitted, so they wouldn't run away.' Frank responded, 'What about brake failure?' He still refused a banker so Frank phoned Control and his request was granted.

At one period during the war, Frank Staddon was relief porter at Kelston station 4 miles west of Bath. He was on the 6.00 p.m. to 10.00 p.m. shift, when one dark evening the station became brilliantly illuminated – a German plane had dropped a flare, which slowly descended and appeared to hang over the last coach of the final train of the day. The terrified guard, expecting every moment to be bombed, or machine-gunned, quickly waved the train off. This was most unfortunate for Frank because he normally caught it home and therefore had to walk along the railway to his home at Bath.

Sometimes traffic was at saturation level on north to south routes. In 1941 John Stamp remembers booking on at 6.35 p.m. on a Tuesday to work the 7.45 p.m. Bath to Birmingham, Washwood Heath freight. It made quite good progress until reaching

Spetchley, 70 miles distant, at 2.00 a.m. on Wednesday. Here it was backed into the Up refuge siding, the signalman warning, 'You're going to be here for a *very* long time.' How right he was – they did not move off for about thirteen hours. During long waits the firebox was shut down, i.e. the dampers were closed and the fire banked to stop the safety valves blowing off, which allowed the crew to rest as best they could on a rather uncomfortable footplate. It moved on 4 miles to Dunhampstead and waited there for half an hour, then continued for another couple of miles to Droitwich Road, where there was a further half hour's delay. At Stoke Works Junction, where the double track became quadruple, the signalman gave the green flag and called, 'There's one up in front and five in front of him,' meaning there were six goods trains in front.

Bromsgrove was reached at 9.30 p.m., about twenty-six hours after leaving Bath. As far as the eye could see trains stood on both Up and Down Main and Slow lines: freight trains,

Class 2P 4–4–0 No. 40509, sister engine of No. 499, with a Down train at Midsomer Norton.

11.5.54 Revd Alan Newman

BR Standard Class 5 4–6–0 No. 73047 passes Kelston station, which closed 1 January 1949 and is seen here in the process of being demolished.

26.8.54 Author

mineral trains, coal trains, petrol trains and ammunition trains. On the Up lines there were mostly empty trains. It had to wait an hour for a banker to assist them up the double-track Lickey Incline. At Barnt Green it passed on to the four-road section, the signalman there giving it the green light at about 11.00 p.m., and were behind six trains which stretched from Barnt Green to King's Norton. The latter was reached at about 4.00 a.m. on Thursday. It stood there and eventually a couple of men arrived at about 6.30 a.m. to relieve them. In all the men had been on duty for a total of 36 hours. The relief crews had arrived in an engine and brake van and this took the Bath men to Saltley where they informed the foreman that, although they were supposed to lodge there, in actual fact they were returning to Bath by passenger train as they had been on duty for 37 hours and had eaten all their food ration.

Driver Edgar Gray had a similar experience. He left Bath at 9.15 p.m. on a Friday and did not arrive at Saltley to hook off until Saturday afternoon. He was allowed eight hours

A train of Up mineral empties approaches Blackwell behind 4–4–0 No. 457.

c. 1917 Author's collection

off duty and returning on Saturday night experienced a good run south as far as Bromsgrove. He was given a Red Alert at Abbots Wood Junction, where he was shunted into the Down refuge siding in order to let the Mail, which was travelling via Worcester, overtake him. While he was waiting he heard a distant 'bang', which was a landmine that had been dropped on the line at Eckington, 6 miles away. As the railway was blocked, he remained in the siding for the whole of the Sunday. When he eventually reached Cheltenham on Monday morning, he was relieved by another crew and returned home as a passenger, arriving at Bath at about 11.00 a.m.

During the Second World War, Control did not dream of relieving men unless they had been on duty for at least twelve hours, simply because men were not available. It was not at all unusual for a Birmingham man working for example from Burton-on-Trent to Gloucester to be relieved at Saltley Junction, go home and have his rest, return for duty and find the same train at the same signal. Some crews became so frustrated that they threw the fire out, walked to the nearest station and caught a train home. This act delayed any train behind it, for if a train in front was dead, it could not be moved.

Travelling extensively, Bath Fireman Doug Holden went away on Monday to Carlisle and did not return home until Thursday. Food rationing caused difficulties at such times, but eventually the motive power depots began to appreciate the problem and supplied

Class 5 4–6–0 No. 44659 passes alongside Saltley station with a Down freight *en route* for St Andrew's.
26.4.58 Michael Mensing

corned beef and biscuits. Doug Holden was eventually called up and sent to the Longmoor Military Railway, Hampshire, for training before being posted to India. After just nine days there, an officer said, 'All up to "H" fall out and go back to your depot' – this was because there was a shortage of crews in Britain. During the war, between Birmingham and Barnt Green two or three trains were coupled to form one train and the permissive block system allowed several freight trains together. The signalman at a preceding box showed the driver a green flag and cautioned him so he knew that somewhere in front there was another train halted. At King's Norton there might be as many as nine trains stopped one behind the other at a signal. As one train went down into Birmingham, those behind moved up to the signal one by one. In the Down direction it was not unusual to take eight hours to travel the dozen miles from Saltley Junction to Barnt Green.

Class 5 4–6–0 No. 44691 and BR Standard Class 9F 2–10–0 No. 92138, the latter being prepared for

work, in Saltley shed.

22.11.64 Michael Mensing

In 1944 specials carried United States' troops and Australian and Canadian airmen from Liverpool docks to Bournemouth. As Bath LMS station was a terminus, while two engines were being hooked on to what had been the rear, the toilets were refilled with water. At some point further north, hundreds of pre-packed meals had been locked in the brake van and after leaving Bath, were distributed throughout the train by trolleys. The greaseproof cardboard boxes contained coffee, dried milk, sugar, half a loaf of bread, butter, Spam or other tinned meat, sweets and chocolate. These empty boxes thrown from the windows littered the line between Bath and Bournemouth. On arrival it was the fireman's job to take a sack and go through the train collecting unused boxes of food and spare tins – a wonderful gleaning in those days of civilian rationing. The food collected was shared among the other staff at Bath shed.

Fireman Fred Epps recounted,

Before D-Day all the way from Masbury to Poole was one mass of stores – you'd never seen anything like it in your life. We ran petrol trains to Masbury. They had thousands and thousands of jerry cans stacked there in the fields round the station and prisoners from Shepton Mallet gaol worked there shifting them. The original siding at Masbury station had more sidings added to it, but after D-Day they were nearly all removed.

Masbury station, view Down. To the left of the telegraph pole can be seen a gate across the War Department siding.

31.7.59 Author

Class 7F 2–8–0 No. 53806 emerges from Devonshire Tunnel with the 12.35 p.m. freight from Bath.

13.11.54 R.E. Toop

From Stourpaine to beyond Blandford all along the roadside you could see guns and tanks, but after D-Day they were gone. It was an amazing sight. It was a marvellous feat how they cleared all the stuff away. At Holes Bay, Poole, you could walk across from one side of the bay to the other on the boats that were in there. It was truly remarkable.

About three or four days before D-Day we pulled into Poole. We had to go to the yard for some reason and got right alongside General Eisenhower's command train. We pulled up almost beside the dining car. We'd never seen such grub for years – chicken, corn on the cob – all piled high by the coloured cooks. My mate said to one of them, 'How about a bit of that then, son?' The smell of the food was delicious.

Ron Gray's worst experience was the first time he drove as a passed fireman. It was a very hot afternoon in June 1944. As usual, it was practice for a young driver to be on the train engine and a senior driver on the assisting engine at the front. At Bath he found he could only get 15 in on the vacuum brake instead of 21 in. Ron went back and inspected his train to see if he could discover any leakage, but found none. On returning to the cab the gauge showed 21 in. The engine was steaming perfectly, so he knew that a locomotive fault was unlikely to be the cause. They set off from Bath and turned on to

Midford station, which is situated on a hillside shelf.

19.8.59 Author

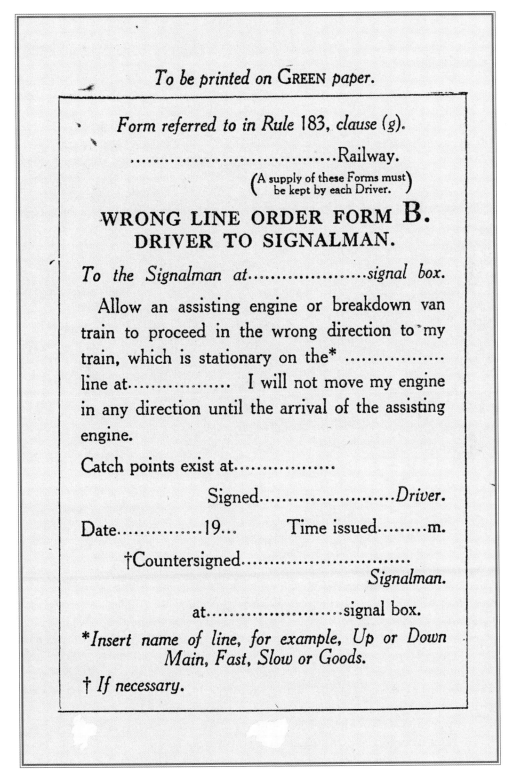

To be printed on GREEN *paper.*

Form referred to in Rule 183, clause (g).

....Railway.

$\left(\begin{array}{c}\text{A supply of these Forms must}\\\text{be kept by each Driver.}\end{array}\right)$

WRONG LINE ORDER FORM B.
DRIVER TO SIGNALMAN.

To the Signalman at.....................signal box.

Allow an assisting engine or breakdown van train to proceed in the wrong direction to my train, which is stationary on the*.................... line at.................... I will not move my engine in any direction until the arrival of the assisting engine.

Catch points exist at....................

        Signed.......................*Driver.*

Date..............19...   Time issued.........m.

†Countersigned....................

                    Signalman.

    at.....................signal box.

*Insert name of line, for example, Up or Down Main, Fast, Slow or Goods.

† If necessary.

A sample 'Wrong Line Order Form' as printed in the Rule Book.

Green Park station, Bath, with Class 2 2–6–2T No. 41240 heading a train for Bristol.

26.8.54 Author

the Somerset & Dorset line. Passing through the single-bore Devonshire Tunnel the engine proceeded only very slowly. The fumes and heat experienced were terrible – the temperature was 80°F even before the two engines added to it. The locomotives were now moving so slowly that they were almost stationary. The driver of the leading engine worked his way back along his tender, then beside Ron's boiler to the footplate and asked why they were going so slowly. Ron was unable to offer any explanation.

At Midford they stopped because the brakes were on. The source of the problem was eventually located: the United States' soldiers had tied their kit bags to the communication cord. They completely failed to understand the problem they were causing and pelted Ron with chewing gum when he asked them politely to take their bags off. They proceeded to the advanced starting signal at Midford and then, because the communication cord had been pulled, stopped again. The footplatemen persuaded the guard to go through the train and explain the problem to the commanding officer, who also did not understand the difficulties his troops were causing. The delays caused the train to arrive at Templecombe 1½ hours late.

Wartime conditions resulted in shortages. 'Wrong Line Orders' were colour-coded: a signalman's yellow, a driver's green and a guard's pink. Owing to a lack of coloured paper, a driver's form was on white paper overprinted with the word 'green' in the appropriate colour. During the blackout this provided one driver with the opportunity of paying a prostitute at Birmingham New Street with a green Wrong Line Order form instead of a green one pound note. The trick failed to succeed and she waited for him the next night and collected her money.

Driver Bert Perry and Fireman Fred Epps, while on the return trip of the 6.30 a.m. passenger from Bath to Bristol, St Philip's, at Mangotsfield picked up a van from a Down express. After arriving at Bath, they shunted the van against the stop block. The delivery van of Broadhurst's, the fish merchants, came to collect the contents but when the railway van door was opened, herrings poured out all over the platform. Instead of being packed in boxes, they had just been thrown in loose with blocks of ice. Railwaymen flocked around with buckets and other containers to help pick up the fish and were able to take some home to supplement their meagre wartime food rations.

Bath LMS station staff near the buffer stops, *c.* 1939.

M.J. Tozer collection

Class 2P 4–4–0 No. 40505 in charge of a Bournemouth West to Templecombe train approaches Shillingstone.

9.9.50 Pursey Short

Evercreech Junction, view Up with the goods yard in the background.

30.10.56 Author

Chapter Four

'FOREIGN' LOCOMOTIVES DURING THE SECOND WORLD WAR

Early in the Second World War, most Class 5 4–6–0s were removed from the Somerset & Dorset to be used elsewhere. Class 4P Compound 4–4–0 No. 1046 was sent as a replacement in September 1941 and the Southern Railway supplied Drummond S11 Class 4–4–0s Nos 395–404 and T9 Class No. 304 of the same wheel arrangement. These were surplus to SR requirements due to the wartime reduction of passenger trains. Although considered easy riding engines, they were thought of as somewhat primitive. Fred Epps fired on one that slipped to a standstill climbing the 1 in 50 out of Bath and it had to return to seek assistance. Their dry sanding did not always function and could cause problems for Up trains in the vicinity of Evercreech New. They primed easily, so a fireman had to watch carefully the water level in the boiler. The steam reverser was a bugbear and when the cut-off was reduced it sometimes went into reverse gear.

Fireman John Stamp considered the Southern Railway 4–4–0s marvellous engines for steam. On passenger trains, and this was the duty for which they were designed, they

Class 4 Compound 4–4–0 No. 1000, the sister engine of No. 1046, at Gloucester MPD. Class 5 2–6–0 No. 2767 is seen in the background.

June 1947 Roger Venning

Drummond S11 Class 4–4–0 No. 404.

c. 1939 Lens of Sutton

could handle three to four coaches, but as they were only equipped with the vacuum brake they were hopeless on freight duty. Although not used on heavy goods trains, they worked lighter ones between Bath and Westerleigh Sidings, north of Bristol. On such duties they needed careful handling or a train's weight would push the engine past an adverse signal. It was not unknown for one to stall on the rising gradient of 1 in 121 between Warmley and Mangotsfield South Junction. Although the 4–4–0s were sometimes used on Somerset & Dorset freight trains, the brakes were insufficient. Harry Whitaker, District Locomotive Superintendent, said to Driver Fred Holmes one day, 'You can take 20 minerals over.' Fred replied, 'Yes, if I have the brakes down on 19 of them.' At least Fred managed to take two ash wagons from Shepton Mallet to the viaduct without encountering any problems.

In April 1942 No. 395, No. 396 and No. 402 were transferred to Saltley for local goods turns and their temporary LMS 2P classification was changed in chalk to 2F. In

T9 Class 4–4–0 No. 30706, on the left, at Bath with the 7.05 p.m. to Bournemouth West. Class 2 2–6–2T No. 41208 stands to the right with the 7.03 p.m. to Bristol Temple Meads, which ran non-stop to Mangotsfield.

26.4.58 R.E. Toop

May 1943 No. 395 and No. 396 were shedded at Burton-on-Trent and, together with No. 397, moved to Peterborough in September 1944. No. 395 was observed on a goods train at Giggleswick on the Settle and Carlisle line on 10 March 1944.

Southern Railway K10 Class 4–4–0 No. 137 on loan to Gloucester shed once appeared on the 10.30 p.m. Bath to Bristol goods with about thirty wagons in tow. Working round the curve and adverse gradient between Mangotsfield South Junction and the station, it reached an accommodation crossing which enabled cattle to pass from a field on one side of the line to the other. Unfortunately, this crossing was plastered with mud and cow dung, causing No. 137 to slip badly so the driver closed the regulator. Unnoticed, the steam reversing gear fell into back gear so that when the driver opened the regulator, the train reversed. Quite unaware that he was going in the wrong direction as blackout sheeting encased the cab, he was surprised to find his train derailed at the trap points protecting the South Junction.

K10 Class 4–4–0 No. 389 at Yeovil Town shed.

c. 1947 W. Hardin Osborne

Class 5 4–6–0 No. 73139 enters Mangotsfield station from the South Junction.

c. 1960 R.J. Cannon/Author's collection

London & North Eastern Railway B12 Class 4–6–0 No. 8577 at Liverpool Street.

12.6.37 J. Hobbs/Author's collection

Ex-GWR 'Dean Goods' 0–6–0, War Department No. 179, formerly ex-GWR No. 2466, at Bath. After the Second World War it was believed to have been sent to China.

1943 John Stamp

War Department 2–10–0 No. 600 *Gordon* at Rainhill celebrating the 150th anniversary of the Liverpool & Manchester Railway.

24.5.80 Author

London & North Eastern Railway 'B12' Class 4–6–0s worked loaded ambulance trains over the S&D, these trains being equipped with Westinghouse brakes. On arrival at Templecombe from the SR, a vacuum brake-fitted LMS engine, or sometimes an SR engine on loan to the LMS, assisted between Templecombe Upper and Bath. As the brakes were incompatible, the LMS drivers were given instructions not to touch the brakes, though if a signal was at danger they did apply them gently in case the LNER driver had failed to observe it.

In about 1943 an ex-GWR 'Dean Goods' 0–6–0, War Department No. 179, formerly GWR No. 2466, passed through Bath LMS *en route* from the north to Blandford Camp, an LMS driver conducting it to Blandford. In about 1944 a War Department 2–10–0 worked a night goods southwards from the Midlands to Bath. When a Bath fireman boarded it at Gloucester and went to fill the tender with water, he found he could not

A crew are manually turning ex-S&DJR Class 4F 0–6–0 No. 44558 at Bath MPD. BR Standard Class 9F

2–10–0 No. 92214 stands in the background.

7.6.64 Author

The leather water hose can be seen to the left of Class 0F 0–4–0T No. 41535 at Gloucester Eastgate.
16.5.59 R.E. Toop

get the large leather bag in. Further investigation revealed that a sieve was causing the problem. He removed it, filled the tender and restored the sieve. No ashpan or dampers were fitted and if you wanted to close the fire down, you had to open the firehole door. The Bath men were impressed by its smooth running, the three braking systems – air, vacuum and steam – and the fact that you could sit down to turn on the injectors. Turning this lengthy machine at Bath, the crew heard a few bumps, but failed to realise their significance. Later they discovered that the buffers had knocked about ten brass handles from SR coaches standing on an adjacent line. Subsequently a notice appeared warning men to be careful when turning a 2–10–0. It returned north the following evening on the 9.15 p.m. goods to Water Orton.

Chapter Five

PUSH-PULL WORKING

In about 1944 Driver Bert Perry and Fireman Fred Epps, and Fireman Len West and another driver, were sent from Bath to the Stonehouse to Stroud and Nailsworth branch to learn how to operate a push-pull train. This was because an aircraft factory had opened at Yate and to carry workers to and from this establishment 'motor train' operation was thought to be the most convenient method as services were to terminate at Wickwar and this station lacked the run-round facilities required by conventional passenger trains. The 'motor train's' driving trailer and two third-class coaches offered a seating capacity of about 286.

The early morning service ran from Bath to Bristol St Philip's and after about an hour's wait ran to Yate and Wickwar with aircraft factory workers. It returned 'empty

Class 1P 0–4–4T No. 1303 at Nailsworth with a push-pull train.

October 1946 W. Potter

A push-pull to Walsall and Wolverhampton leaving Streetly station pushed by Class 2 2–6–2T No. 41220.
4.8.57 Michael Mensing

coaching stock' to St Philip's, where the coaches were stabled. The engine collected the Newcastle mail coaches from the carriage sidings there and took them to Mangotsfield to turn on the triangle. Turning was essential as the mail pick-up and dropping apparatus was only on one side. Following its return to Bristol, it ran 'empty coaching stock' to Wickwar and called at all stations back to Bristol St Philip's. Later in the evening it ran from St Philip's to Bath. On Sundays, the set was used more intensively. It ran from Bath to Bristol Temple Meads, as St Philip's was closed on Sundays, and then ran to Wickwar. It returned empty to Temple Meads and worked the mid-morning train to Bath. In the late afternoon it ran from Bath to Temple Meads via Wickwar. Then it returned and later made a trip to Mangotsfield and back to connect with trains to and from the north.

View Up at Wickwar station.

11.5.61 Author

The Class 1P 0–4–4T working this duty left Bath shed bunker-first and coupled to the coaches with the engine at the Bath end of the train. The two vacuum pipes on the motor-fitted engine had different pattern ends so that it was impossible to couple the vacuum brake pipe to the vacuum-worked regulator pipe. Twin cylinders beside the smoke box cut steam off, or applied it. The fireman, apart from attending to the fire and water, was required to adjust the cut-off, and initially open the regulator. He also had to turn on the blower to avoid a blow-back when his driver closed the regulator. Electric-bell communication was provided between the driver's vestibule on the coach and the engine cab. At first ordinary passenger link firemen were used until it was realised that when the fireman was alone on the footplate he held such serious responsibilities that he must be a passed fireman.

Drivers found that the skills learnt on the footplate could not always be transferred to a control vestibule. Standing at the front of a coach with sleepers whizzing by just beneath you made it more difficult to judge speed and a driver

View Down at Warmley station.

c. 1910 M.J. Tozer collection

tended either to shut off steam too late, or too early and maybe had to set back, or draw forward.

One driver allowed his mate to fire and drive the engine, the driver giving all his attention to operating the brake and observing both the signals and lady guard. A problem experienced when pushing a train on a cold morning was that steam leaking from the heating hose at the leading end of the train tended to douse the headlamp. If possible an SR headlamp was used on this duty as this pattern seemed less prone to trouble.

A daredevil driver drove an engine out of Bath shed by standing beside the smoke box of a push-pull equipped locomotive and controlling it from the vacuum pump of the motor apparatus. Another dangerous practice when shunting an engine single-handed at the Bath shed was to drive it up the steep incline away from the depot; jump from it as it slowed down; change the points and as it drifted back down by gravity, jump back on and regain the cab. Had that person slipped, the engine may have passed over him, or run out of control.

One driver of a push-pull train found that his brakes would not work at Lawrence Hill Junction, just outside of Bristol St Philip's station, so he kept ringing the bell indicating to his fireman to reverse the engine. Fortunately, he complied. On another occasion a push-pull failed to start from Warmley towards Mangotsfield because a buffer had become caught in a level crossing gate.

Motor fitted Class 1P 0–4–4T No. 1348 at Saltley shed.

24.9.32 R.J. Essery collection

11

RUNNING TIMES FOR FREIGHT TRAINS

POINTS BETWEEN.	Minutes.	POINTS BETWEEN.	Minutes.
Bath Yard	—	Bournemouth West	—
Bath Junction	1	Poole	16
Midford	14	Broadstone	12
Wellow	8	Corfe Mullen Junction	10
Radstock	12	Bailey Gate	5
Midsomer Norton	10	Blandford	15
Chilcompton	10	Shillingstone	14
Binegar	10	Sturminster Newton	9
Masbury	7	Stalbridge	11
Shepton Mallet	9	Henstridge	6
Evercreech New	13	Templecombe No. 2	7
Evercreech Junction North	4	Templecombe Lower	8
Evercreech Junction	2	Templecombe No. 2	—
Cole	10	Templecombe Upper	2
Wincanton to	15	Wincanton	10
Templecombe Lower	10	Cole	12
Wincanton to	—	Evercreech Junction	10
Templecombe Upper	11	Evercreech Junction North	2
Wincanton to	10	Evercreech New	5
Templecombe No. 2	10	Shepton Mallet	17
Templecombe Upper	2	Masbury	11
Templecombe Lower	10	Binegar	7
Templecombe No. 2 to	—	Chilcompton	7
Henstridge	7	Midsomer Norton	7
Stalbridge	6	Radstock	7
Sturminster Newton	11	Wellow	10
Shillingstone	9	Midford	8
Blandford	14	Bath Junction	14
Bailey Gate	15	Bath Yard	1
Corfe Mullen Junction	5		
Broadstone	10		
Poole	10		
Bournemouth West	16		

POINTS BETWEEN.	Minutes.	POINTS BETWEEN.	Minutes.
Evercreech Junction North	—	Burnham	—
Pylle	6	Highbridge Wharf	5
West Pennard	10	Highbridge Station	3
Glastonbury	12	Bason Bridge	5
		Edington Junction	10
Wells	—		
Glastonbury	18	Edington Junction	—
		Bridgwater	23
Glastonbury	—		
Ashcott	8	Edington Junction	—
Shapwick	5	Shapwick	7
Edington Junction	7	Ashcott	5
		Glastonbury	8
Bridgwater	—		
Edington Junction	23	Glastonbury	—
		Polsham	9
Edington Junction	—	Wells	8
Bason Bridge	10		
Highbridge Station	5	Glastonbury	—
Highbridge Wharf	3	West Pennard	13
Burnham	5	Pylle	14
		Evercreech Junction North	6

Extract from the Somerset & Dorset Joint Committee working timetable of freight trains from 1 October 1945.

Chapter Six

The Author Travels Over the Mendips on the Footplate and in a Brake Van

On 31 August 1960, with my footplate pass safely in my pocket, I waited patiently on Bath Green Park station for the arrival of the 9.03 a.m. from Bristol, Temple Meads. The coaches of this train were composed of Southern Region stock and worked through to Bournemouth West. As Green Park was a terminus, the engine that was to take it on to Bournemouth had to come from the shed and be coupled on to what was the rear of the train.

As the engine approached, I noticed it had a BR Standard tender and casually assumed it to be a Class 4 or Class 5. As it drew closer my excitement knew no bounds when I saw that it was BR Standard Class 9 2–10–0 No. 92204, a type that had only recently been introduced to the S&D line. Although really freight engines, they had been found to be successful on passenger duties and had in fact attained a speed of 90 mph, not that such speeds were expected over the S&D. Class 9s were able to draw passenger trains of 410 tons unassisted, compared with the maximum of 270 tons for Class 5s, or Bulleid Light Pacifics, and 320 tons for the S&D Class 7F 2–8–0s. This meant that a 2–10–0 did not require an assisting engine over the Mendips saving both locomotives and manpower, often hard to come by on a busy summer Saturday. The four coaches, therefore, were a very puny load for the Class 9F, the most powerful of the BR Standard locomotives.

BR Standard Class 9 2–10–0 No. 92204 at Bath Green Park backing on to the 9.53 a.m. to Bournemouth West.

31.8.60 Author

I made myself known to Inspector McArthy who was to accompany me, and in turn he introduced me to Driver Gunning and Fireman Ryle. I had barely time to settle myself in the cab before the regulator was opened and we were off, five minutes late. With such a light load, No. 92204 accelerated quickly past Bath motive power depot and we were on the single line, the fireman leaning out to take the tablet from Whitaker's catcher. We pounded up the 1 in 50 gradient at a steady 25 mph and curved round overlooking the crescents of Bath. I had expected the fireman to be continuously at work, but noticed that he only needed to put on six shovelsful of brickettes at the foot of the gradient and another six before we entered Devonshire Tunnel about 2 miles from Green Park station.

Beyond the tunnel we experienced a 10 mph check over a weak underbridge in Lyncombe Vale and so entered the mile-long Combe Down Tunnel at slow speed. As

BR Standard Class 9 2–10–0 No. 92204 at Bath MPD.

30.6.60 Revd Alan Newman

No. 92214, a sister engine to No. 92204 on which the author travelled, having ashes raked from the firebox at Bath, its home shed.

c. 1960 Dr T.R.N. Edwards

the tunnel was low and the Class 9's chimney not far from the roof, the smoke beat down on us and I took the precaution of breathing through my handkerchief. The whistle sounded harsh in the tunnel and as we gathered speed down the gradient of 1 in 100, the noise, vibration and dryness gave me a feeling of elation, tinged with a touch of nervousness, such as I have felt when standing at the stern of a vessel in a rough sea.

Feeling rather relieved, we came out of the tunnel and rounded the curves to Midford where the fireman placed the tablet in Whitaker's apparatus. After the tablet had been caught he lifted the catcher off the tender and laid it on the cab floor as it was not wanted again until the next single line section began at Templecombe.

Six more shovelsful were put on at Midford and again beyond Wellow. Steam was blowing from the safety valves before we reached Radstock only two minutes behind schedule. We left Radstock up the 1 in 55 and at 20 mph climbed the side of the valley

The gradient post at Bath Junction indicating 1 in 50.

c. December 1965 C. Steane

Whitaker's delivery apparatus at Midford
signal-box.

c. December 1965 C. Steane

BR Standard Class 9 2–10–0 No. 92203 just beyond Midford with the 2.50 p.m. Bath to Bournemouth West.

10.9.60 Author

Binegar station, view Down.

December 1965 C. Steane

The derelict Winsor Hill signal-box, which closed on 3 August 1948. The entrance to the Down tunnel is seen immediately to the right of the signal-box.

31.7.59 Author

at 1 in 50 until we were above a row of miners' cottages. We passed Old Pit, sunk in 1763 and once facetiously referred to as 'Lord Chatham'. More brickettes were shovelled on at Midsomer Norton and we left only half a minute late.

The weather looked more stormy as we climbed into the Mendips. Chilcompton was left on time and we rapidly accelerated to 20 mph. I noticed with interest that through quite a large gap between the firebox and the cab floor I could see the last coupled wheel and the track. The cab roof was so low that when I stood upright I could see over the top. Despite the massive boiler, when seated, visibility was surprisingly good through the front window.

On the level stretch at Binegar speed rose to 36 mph. The brickettes were very dusty so the fireman was kept busy operating the tender spray and making sure there was

BR Standard Class 5 4–6–0 No. 73054 and Class 9 2–10–0 No. 92245 work through Midsomer

Norton with the Down 'Pines Express'. Notice the greenhouse beside the signal-box that was used for growing plants for the station garden.

3.7.62 Author's collection

The Bath Road Viaduct following its partial collapse on 2 February 1946.

Author's collection

sufficient water to keep the dust down without us having to paddle on the footplate. On one occasion a flood did flow from the tender and in the nick of time I placed my none too waterproof shoes on an upturned bucket. The floor soon dried and the fireman brushed it as conscientiously as a houseproud wife.

We gained Masbury Summit 811 ft above sea level and were soon rushing down the 1 in 50 at 50–60 mph while enjoying an extensive view over the Vale of Avalon towards Glastonbury Tor and beyond. The rocking of the engine caused the brickettes to roll forward to the footplate and the fireman had to shovel them up. To prevent flames from the firebox blowing back into the cab, he closed the dampers before we entered the twin-bore Winsor Hill Tunnel and, on its approach, warned me to close my eyes. I was glad I took his advice because I felt stinging blows as coal dust blew up into my face.

BR Standard Class 9 2–10–0 No. 92204 at Evercreech Junction with the 9.53 a.m. Bath to Bournemouth West.

31.8.60 Author

We rocked over the 118–yd–long Bath Road Viaduct and the 308–yd–long Charlton Viaduct and came to rest at Shepton Mallet station. We left on time, climbed out of Shepton and drifted down to Evercreech New enjoying another fine view, though less extensive than that from Masbury. All too soon we passed Evercreech Junction North signal-box and drew to a standstill at Evercreech Junction where I reluctantly left No. 92204.

My return to Bath was on the 1.50 p.m. goods from Evercreech Junction. Ex-S&D Class 7F 2–8–0 No. 53805 had worked out with the 11.00 a.m. goods from Bath. As I climbed into the cab I noticed how open and airy it was compared with that of No. 92204, an improvement on a hot day, but not so pleasant if the weather was cold, wet or windy. Through a window I could look over the top of the firebox, the sides of which were upright and not sloping as those of No. 92204; also the cab offered much more headroom. We had a light load of fourteen 'cripples' for repair at Radstock Wagon Works and four minutes early, started the 8-mile-climb to Masbury.

The fireman did little firing and was mainly concerned with feeding the boiler with water. 'Give her water and she'll make steam all right,' he said. He was careful to keep the water high in the gauge glass because at Cannard's Grave Cutting when the engine went over the top down towards Shepton Mallet, the water would surge forward and perhaps only show a 'quarter of the glass' in the gauge. In the event, when we passed over the summit, the water only fell to half a glass. Had we been having a rough trip, the drift down into Shepton would have given the fireman an opportunity to right the fire before the long slog up to Masbury.

Passing over Charlton Viaduct I looked down on a most attractive factory garden as we pounded up the 1 in 50 gradient at 12 mph. From Evercreech Junction to Masbury Summit took 29 minutes giving an average speed of about 16 mph. At the summit Driver George Tucker closed the regulator and his fireman opened the blower to keep

Class 7F 2–8–0 No. 53805 arriving at Evercreech Junction.

31.8.60 Author

Class 7F 2–8–0 No. 53805 at Bath MPD.

29.6.57 Revd Alan Newman

the fire bright. We drifted down to Midsomer Norton at 35 mph and beyond the station the brake was gradually applied until speed was reduced to 15 mph to observe a check where the embankment had slipped.

At Radstock the brake van was uncoupled and the wagons shunted for repair. The guard informed us that the Radstock Class 3F 0–6–0T would push our load to the main line, so No. 53805 moved to the Up road where we waited. After a few minutes the signalman beckoned us back again. Apparently, the driver of the Radstock shunter wanted No. 53805 to draw out the wagons so that as soon as we drew them forward he could make a dash for the shed and go off duty. We drew the fourteen wagons, mostly loaded with coal, from in front of the Class 3F, dropped them back on to our brake van and set off for Bath. Our load was very small compared with what it would have been in previous years and it was sad to pass derelict mine and quarry sidings indicating that the industry was being run down.

Charlton Viaduct, view towards Masbury.

1966 C. Steane

Soon we were passing through Wellow at 27 mph and as we drew to a halt at Midford's outer home signal, the first portion of the Down 'Pines Express' passed on the other line. The fireman phoned to the signal-box (Rule 55 [see p. 143] did not have to be carried out as the track circuit prevented any dangerous conflicting movements), and was informed that we would be held there until the 3.20 p.m. Bath to Templecombe came off the single line section ahead. The fireman had been keeping the fire low purposely as it had to be dropped on arrival at Bath and to make it an easier task for the lad who was to carry out this procedure, he raked through the fire. Meanwhile, I listened to delightful tales of rough trips.

The second part of the 'Pines' went by followed by the 3.20 p.m. We set off, accelerating rapidly down over the viaduct to get a run at the gradient up to Combe Down Tunnel and we were inside almost before I had my handkerchief out. As the smoke was higher above my head than with a Class 9, I found it more convenient to stand with my back to the firebox and not use my handkerchief at all because the air was

The Up outer home and calling-on arm, Midford.

15.8.59 Author

A 57XX Class 0–6–0PT shunting at Bath.

c. 1962 R.J. Cannon/Author's collection

quite breathable. It seemed to take a long time going up through the tunnel and I watched the glow from the partially opened firebox door flickering on the tunnel roof. I stared ahead, the tunnel seeming to go on for ever.

At last we rounded a curve and there before us was the tunnel mouth. We emerged slowly ready for the 10 mph speed restriction. We went through Devonshire Tunnel and cautiously descended the bank into Bath, the fireman placing the tablet in the catcher and sliding it out ready to be received. In the shunting neck an ex-GWR 0–6–0PT was ready to shunt the train and we proceeded to the turntable in a steady drizzle, my day's excitement over.

★   ★   ★

Class 4F No. 44146 at Bath ready to bank the 11.00 a.m. goods to Evercreech Junction as far as Combe Down Tunnel.

5.9.60 Author

Less than a week later, on 5 September 1960, the author was privileged to be able to take a brake van trip on the 11.00 a.m. goods from Bath to Evercreech Junction with Guard Ted Elkins. Arriving at the stationmaster's office, Bath Green Park, Stationmaster Peter Pearman escorted me along the track to Midland Road Sidings, where I was pleased to learn that the train I would be travelling on had more than twenty-three wagons, which meant that it required banking assistance up the 1 in 50 gradient to Combe Down Tunnel.

I climbed into the van and Class 4F 0–6–0 No. 44146 drew the train of twenty-five wagons out of the siding and the train engine, BR Standard Class 5 4–6–0 No. 73047, backed on to the front, No. 44146 remaining at the other end to act as banker. Its smokebox dominated the rear view from the brake van. After an exchange of 'crow' whistles, both drivers opened their regulators simultaneously.

BR Standard Class 5 No. 73047 climbing the 1 in 50 out of Bath with the 11.00 a.m. goods to

We crossed the lines leading to Mangotsfield and at Bath Junction signal-box the train engine fitted with Whitaker's apparatus collected the tablet automatically and the fireman quickly retrieved it. As No. 44146 passed, the signalman hooked the loop of the banking staff case over the fireman's arm. Now on the gradient of 1 in 50, we laboured through the suburbs of Bath at a steady 18 mph, No. 44146 pounding away noisily behind us as, from the guard's van veranda, I enjoyed the view of the city spread out before me.

When we reached the 447-yd-long, single-bore Devonshire Tunnel, I took Guard Elkins' advice and moved inside the van for the trip through the tunnel. I was very glad I did, and even inside, the fumes seeped through cracks in the doorway and filled the van making the atmosphere look as if it had been polluted by a crowd of smokers. As soon as we reached daylight, I returned to the veranda to gasp fresh air. I was able to enjoy this

Evercreech Junction.

13.10.61 R.E. Toop

for just over ⅓ mile as we climbed through Lyncombe Vale, the exhaust from the two engines reverberating in this steep-sided valley.

I felt a jerk as No. 44146 dropped off at the entrance to the mile-long Combe Down Tunnel and No. 73047 took the weight of the whole train.

It grew dark very rapidly as the low tunnel filled with smoke. At a point 220 yds beyond the tunnel mouth the gradient changed to 1 in 100 down and there was a shriek as Guard Elkins screwed down his handbrake and further shrieks from the protesting brake blocks as he tightened it. It sounded most eerie in the absolute darkness until I realised what had caused the noise.

Midford is in a dip and passing over the 132-yd-long viaduct, Guard Elkins released the brakes as the train charged up the 1 in 60. Skill was necessary to know when to take the brakes off, because if he had released them too early, and the buffers been under

Class 4F 0–6–0 No. 44096 banks a goods train out of Bath and approaches Devonshire Tunnel.

1.9.52 R.E. Toop

compression, the couplings would have snatched and a link may well have broken, thus dividing the train. I was interested to learn that Guard Elkins told me that the signalman at Bath Junction often gets the 'out of section' bell from Midford box just as he goes out to collect the staff from the returning banker.

Descending the 1 in 106 to Wellow, speed rose to 23 mph and Guard Elkins screwed down his brake. He released it on the flatter stretch through the station and screwed it down again as speed rose to 34 mph down the 1 in 132. Speed increased as we rushed through Shoscombe & Single Hill Halt at 39 mph, but our progress was soon impeded and I felt a bump as the buffers struck each other when Driver Harry Starkey closed the regulator, for the Writhlington distant signal was 'on'. Guard Elkins remarked that it was fortunate that the empty box vans were near the rear of the train. Had they been in front and the loaded coal wagons behind them, the trip would have been much rougher.

The stop at Writhlington was caused because at Radstock an Up goods had been shunted across our path to allow the Up 'Pines Express' to overtake it. As soon as

Class 4F 0–6–0 No. 44146 banking a freight train through Lyncombe Vale. Class 7F 2–8–0 No. 53803 was the train engine.

13.11.54 R.E. Toop

No. 44146 dropped off at the entrance to the mile-long Combe Down Tunnel.

5.9.60 Author

Class 7F 2–8–0 No. 53804 approaching Midford with a Down train.

19.8.59 Author

The guard's view of No. 73047 climbing south of Midford.

5.9.60 Author

View Up at Wellow station.

20.6.59 Author

we stopped at Writhlington, the guard climbed down and went to the signal-box, to carry out Rule 55. He signed the train register and the signalman counter-signed, so that in the event of our train being run into from the rear, responsibility would have rested with the signalman. Had the fireman been nearer to the box than the guard, he would have carried out the rule. While waiting for the signals to clear, I noticed in the corner of the van a sprag for placing in the spokes (or holes in disc wheels) of wagons with faulty brakes when they needed to be stopped.

The first portion of the 'Pines' passed and then the second. The signal fell and Harry Starkey opened the regulator. No. 73047 slipped and the wagons surged forward and jerked. She soon found her feet as the gradient fell just beyond the signal and we dropped down to Radstock past untidy looking slag heaps.

View Up at Shoscombe and Single Hill Halt.

February 1966 C. Steane

We went under the sloping 'Marble Arch' overbridge, which was being demolished as the siding that also passed under it had such a low clearance that a special low-height Sentinel shunter had to be used to work trains along this siding. The siding passing below the arch was only high enough for an open wagon and on several occasions brake vans had their roofs stripped off trying to pass through it.

At Radstock we stopped for banking assistance up the 7½ miles of 1 in 50/63 to Masbury. Class 3F 0–6–0T No. 47496 drew up behind the brake van, Guard Elkins coupled up and removed our tail lamp. Unlike that which helped us out of Bath, No. 47496 had to be coupled as we needed assistance through several sections. Had it not been coupled, and the banker failed, and we passed through a section with our rear lamp on the van, a signalman could have believed the train complete, signalled it 'Out of section' and the banker struck by a following train. I noticed how much lower the boiler of No. 47496 was compared with that of the Class 4F which had banked us out of Bath.

BR Standard Class 5 4–6–0 No. 73047 at Writhlington, as seen from the brake van.

5.9.60 Author

We climbed at 1 in 50 parallel with the ex-GWR's Bristol to Frome branch and climbed over it at 'Five Arches' just as a goods train appeared. We passed Norton Hill Colliery and *Lord Salisbury*, the National Coal Board's 0–6–0ST shunter and went through Midsomer Norton, which had a magnificent display of dahlias in the station garden and an expertly tended lawn; our speed was only 13 mph, so there was plenty of time to admire it.

We accelerated after Moorewood Quarry Sidings and made a momentary stop at Binegar for Guard Elkins to uncouple No. 47496 and replace our tail lamp. Had our van been an older type where the body extended to the headstock, Guard Elkins would have uncoupled on the move (normally within Binegar station limits so that the signalman

145

Loaded coal wagons at Writhlington Colliery.

February 1966 C. Steane

Radstock East signal-box shortly after the line was doubled on 1 July 1894. The low Tyning Bridge can be seen to the right.

c. 1894 Author's collection

Class 3F 0–6–0T No. 47496 approaches the brake van of the 11.00 a.m. Bath to Evercreech Junction goods in order to assist it to Masbury Summit. Radstock engine shed is on the right.

5.9.60 Author

Sentinel 0–4–0 shunter No. 47191 at the 'Marble Arch'. This class of engine was of specially low height in order to pass under this bridge.

26.2.53 Revd Alan Newman

Class 3F 0–6–0T No. 47465, sister engine to No. 47496, at Radstock ready for the 'big push'.

9.11.54 Revd Alan Newman

Class 3F 0–6–0T No. 47496 – the uncoupling hook can be seen suspended from the smokebox handrail.

5.9.60 Author

Class 3F 0–6–0T No. 47465 banking a train at Five Arches. The other three arches are located behind the trees on the left. The line in the foreground is the ex-GWR Radstock to Bristol line.

27.8.53 Author

'Just as a goods train appeared' – No. 47496 approaching Midsomer Norton. To the left in the distance can be seen an ex-GWR 2–8–0T on the Radstock to Bristol line.

5.9.60 Author

Lord Salisbury, a Peckett 0–6–0ST built in 1906, seen here at Norton Hill Colliery.

14.8.59 Author

could see this operation had been carried out), by using a special hook normally hung on the banker's smokebox door. The fireman of No. 47496 collected a staff at Binegar so that his engine could return 'wrong line'.

This banking key caused confusion on one occasion. Two Class 4F 0–6–0s were coupled at the head of a full load towards Masbury with a Class 3F 0–6–0T assisting at the rear. Being double track, the Binegar banking key was put out for the banker only, but the fireman on the leading engine looking ahead and seeing the key in the station apparatus, not thinking clearly, put out his own catcher and remarked to his driver, 'I got'n mate.' It was the only time that the locomotive inspector on the engine had been known to swear and his 'You b—— fool' was immediately followed with, 'I am sorry', from the bottom of his heart. The key was thrown off the leading engine by the errant

'Midsomer Norton which had a magnificent display of dahlias' – an S&DJR 0–6–0 waits by the signal-box at Midsomer Norton. The view is towards Radstock and the well-known dahlia display is clearly seen.

c. 1905 Author's collection

The guard's view of BR Standard Class 5 4–6–0 No. 73047 as it climbs near Chilcompton.

5.9.60 Author

Guard Elkins uncouples Class 3F 0–6–0T No. 47496 at Binegar.

5.9.60 Author

fireman to be lost for hours, and the banker having no key, and therefore no authority to proceed, had to drop off at Binegar leaving the train to crawl over Masbury Summit without banking assistance.

However, we had no such trouble and at Masbury Summit, 811 ft above sea level, I felt a bump as the banker left and the weight of the train was taken by the couplings. Guard Elkins applied his brake before reaching the summit because the wagons towards the front of the train were already descending.

Unfortunately, it was rather a misty day and the view was not as breathtaking as it might have been. Beyond Masbury Halt, speed on the 1 in 50 descent rose to 35 mph and then 36 mph beyond the twin-bore Winsor Hill Tunnels. Guard Elkins screwed down his brake harder as we approached Shepton Mallet as he expected Harry Starkey to stop for water as usual, but as we passed the platform he realised we were not going to halt and so released it. We climbed under the ex-GWR's Witham to Yatton line just as BR Standard Class 3MT 2–6–2T No. 82004 was passing over with a passenger train. Our brake was then applied for the descent of 1 in 50 through Cannard's Grave Cutting, named after the legendary giant reputed to have been buried nearby. The speed rose to 23 mph and then the brake was released for the climb of 1 in 196 to Evercreech Junction North. We stopped, the 'x'-shaped backing signal was pulled off and the train reversed into the sidings.

After I had my sandwich lunch and No. 73047 turned, I climbed into an Eastern Region brake van for the return trip, Guard Elkins remarking that this type of van gave a

Class 3F 0–6–0T No. 47496 drops off at Masbury Summit.

5.9.60 Author

rougher ride. With nineteen empties on we climbed at 21 mph to Evercreech New, but on the 1 in 50 beyond, speed fell to 12 mph. I noticed that the guard always sat on the left facing the engine – this was the same side as the driver – to enable the signals to be better sighted.

Just before Shepton Mallet, Guard Elkins applied the brake and released it again as we went over the impressive 308-yd-long, curving Charlton Viaduct. We seemed to reach Masbury very quickly and before long the brake was applied for the descent the other side and we rattled through Binegar at 31 mph. At Chilcompton, despite the signals being 'off', I was surprised to feel the train stopping. Guard Elkins explained that the driver wanted water. Sure enough, looking out I saw the fireman climbing up on the tender and putting the bag in.

The view Up at Masbury Halt.

December 1965 C. Steane

BR Standard Class 3MT 2–6–2T No. 82004 working a Witham to Yatton stopping train, passes over the 11.00 a.m. Bath to Evercreech Junction goods just south of Shepton Mallet station.

5.9.60 Author

BR Standard Class 5 4–6–0 No. 73047 descends the 1 in 50 over Prestleigh Viaduct.

5.9.60 Author

At Evercreech Junction No. 73047 backs the wagons into a siding.

5.9.60 Author

Guard Elkins on the veranda of the ER brake van at the rear of the 1.50 p.m. freight from
Evercreech Junction to Bath.

5.9.60 Author

BR Standard Class 5 4–6–0 No. 73047 at Evercreech Junction before working the 1.50 p.m. to Bath. Driver

Starkey is lighting a cigarette.

5.9.60 Author

BR Standard Class 5 4–6–0 No. 73047 nears Masbury Summit with the 1.50 p.m. Evercreech Junction to Bath.
5.9.60 Author

At Chilcompton the fireman stands on the tender to supervise filling the tank with water.
5.9.60 Author

BR Standard Class 5 4–6–0 No. 73047, descending between Midsomer Norton and Radstock, crosses No. 53805 with a Bath to Evercreech Junction freight.

5.9.60 Author

At Midsomer Norton No. 73047 took thirteen wagons across to the Down line, ran round them and pushed them to Norton Hill Colliery. Meanwhile, another wagon which had been uncoupled was allowed to run by gravity into the station sidings. The remaining five empties were dropped at Radstock. While No. 73047 was getting out eleven loaded wagons for Bath, it became trapped on the far side of the line until the first portion of the Down 'Pines' had gone by.

Approaching Writhlington, we found the distant signal 'on' and drew up at the home. The signalman instructed us to reverse across the Down line and pull into one of the Down sidings because the second part of the 'Pines' was late. Had we proceeded we would have had to have waited at Midford for it to come off the single line section and in turn we would have held up the 1.08 p.m. from Bournemouth West scheduled to arrive at Bath at 4.22 p.m. We had to wait at Writhlington for it to precede us. The 3.20 p.m. Bath to Templecombe came by before the second portion of the Down 'Pines' which usually preceded it. When the 1.08 p.m. from Bournemouth West passed, we backed out, regained the Up line and continued. The brake was applied as we raced down to Wellow at 39 mph and beyond the station it was released on the rising gradient where speed dropped to 32 mph.

Class 8F 2–8–0 No. 48706 passing the Down sidings, Writhlington.

c. December 1965 C. Steane

Midford distant was 'on' and we waited at the outer home for the 3.35 p.m. service Bristol, Temple Meads to Bournemouth West and the 4.35 p.m. Bath to Templecombe stopping train to clear the single line section ahead. In due course we received the 'right away' and accelerated over the viaduct and through the station, its single platform perched precariously on a cliff ledge. Midford is rather an odd village in having no church and being located in no less than four parishes.

After the 4.35 p.m. had passed, we quickly accelerated over Midford Viaduct and rushed up Park Bank towards Combe Down Tunnel. Inside the tunnel we felt a jerk as No. 73047 slipped, but with only half a load there was little fear that the train would be drawn by gravity backwards out of the tunnel through the same entrance as it went in.

Guard Elkins told me there were ninety-three rail joints in the mile-long tunnel. As the descent into Bath started before reaching the far end of the tunnel, so that he knew when to apply his brake to avoid the van bumping its buffers into the train, he counted seventy-two rail beats and then applied his brake. We cautiously descended the bank into Bath and drew to a halt as the Class 3F 0–6–0T left the shunting spur to draw up to the rear of the train to shunt the wagons. Another day's excitement was over.

Chapter Seven

CREWS' COMMENTS ON SOME LOCOMOTIVE TYPES

CLASS 2P 4–4–0S

At one time a Class 2P hauled the eight-coach 'Pines Express', which included a restaurant car – a heavier vehicle than a normal coach. The engine had to be 'thrashed' from Gloucester to Standish Junction and the injector shut off because all the steam was needed for traction. This meant that by the time Standish Junction was reached, the water level was dangerously low, but there the descent provided the opportunity to refill the boiler. Class 2P 4–4–0s were also used on many of the Bath to Bournemouth West stopping trains. Nos 629, 634 and 696 were exceptional engines, superior to the others and considered masters of their work. Engines of this class worked the 'Pines Express' over the Somerset & Dorset until 1938, taking six coaches including a twelve-wheel dining car, the total weight of the train amounting to over 200 tons.

In November 1933 No. 633 was fitted experimentally with a Dabeg feed water heater pump worked off the return crank on the link motion and mounted on the left-hand platform adjacent to the smokebox. Before being fed into the boiler, water took heat from exhaust steam. The ordinary live steam injector was retained, but the Dabeg heater replaced the exhaust steam injector. Although this heater reduced fuel and water consumption and saved on boiler maintenance, savings were considered insufficient to cover the purchase price of £425. No. 633 retained the heater until its withdrawal.

Class 2P 4–4–0 No. 523 hauls the Down 'Pines Express' through Lyncombe Vale.

1934 Author's collection

Class 2P 4–4–0 No. 40696 near Wellow with an Up stopping train.

14.8.54 R.E. Toop

Class 2P 4–4–0 No. 40634 and BR Standard Class 5 4–6–0 No. 73087 head the Down 'Pines Express' through Midford.

14.8.56 Author

Class 2P 4–4–0 No. 40569 and Class 7F 2–8–0 No. 53810 on the Down line south of Midford.

5.8.61 Author

Class 2P 4–4–0 No. 40652 and BR Standard Class 5 No. 73050 with the 'Pines Express' leave the
Mangotsfield line at Bath Junction and begin the climb to Combe Down Tunnel.

28.10.59 Author

Fireman Fred Epps considered the feed water heater 'a wonderful thing'. On one occasion he turned it on and because it was silent, forgot about it until suddenly water started bubbling up the chimney and warned him that the boiler was getting rather full. No. 633 and No. 634 had patent firebars designed in one piece and could only be removed when the boiler was washed out. This meant that clinker had to be shovelled out.

One day 4–4–0 No. 698 arrived at Bath with the Up 'Pines Express'. Examining it on arrival, Fitter Reg Iley felt something pawing the top of his cap. He found it to be a kitten belonging to the Broadstone shed cat, the animal having travelled on the engine's bogie, which was relatively stable when the engine was in motion. The kitten was found a good home at Bath.

When the Bath Junction Class 3F shunter was temporarily sent to shed, a Class 2P 4–4–0 took over its duties before working a passenger turn. On one occasion the 2.10 p.m. 'engine and van' shunting at Weston had slipped and fractured a coupling rod. The Class 2P on shunting duties was sent to collect it, but while towing it back more

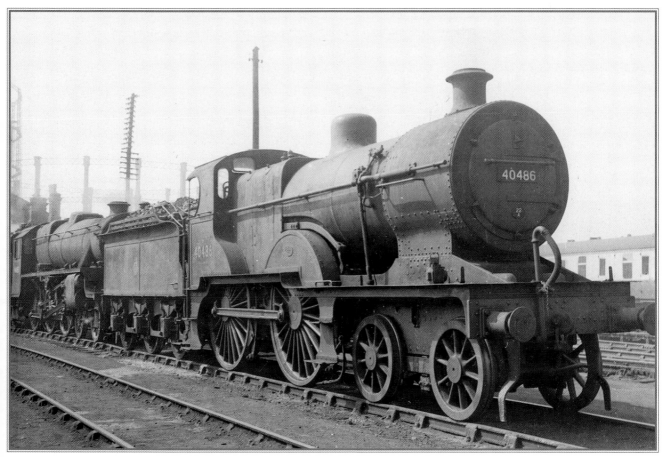

Class 2P 4–4–0 No. 40486 of 22A (Bristol) at its home shed.

21.4.55 Revd Alan Newman

Two Class 2P 4–4–0s head a stopping train near Binegar; No. 633 is the leading engine.

c. 1935 Author's collection

mechanism came loose and fitters had to be sent for. They arrived on their bicycles and rendered it safe to be hauled by the 2P.

If the blower was not turned on before passing through the twin-bore Winsor Hill Tunnel, often at 60 mph, there was a serious risk of the fire being blown back into the cab. The sudden rush of air sometimes forced the cab's floorboards up – the 600 class 4–4–0s being particularly prone to this failure.

To prepare a 'high wheeler', a driver had to place it in exactly the right position on a pit road so that he could get up behind the big ends to withdraw the corks and oil the bearings. One day Albert Williams, who always took great pride in his appearance and whose overalls looked as clean at the end of the week as they did at the beginning, got underneath a 4–4–0 and, as usual, placed his oil can up on the web prior to taking the corks out. Unfortunately, it slipped off, and drenched him with oil, ruining his pristine appearance. Incidentally, the railway provided two sets of bib and brace overalls annually, together with an overall coat, a black jacket and either a mac or an overcoat every other year.

CLASS 4P COMPOUND 4–4–0S

Opinions were mixed regarding the Compounds: some considered them to be excellent machines, while others did not appreciate their qualities. When new in 1924, No. 1065 worked on trials over the S&D and, following bridge reconstruction on the Mangotsfield to Bath line in the 1930s, Compounds were able to run to Bath regularly. No. 1046 replaced one of the Class 5 4–6–0s withdrawn from Bath at the beginning of the Second World War for use elsewhere. One driver never took No. 1046 out of 'simple' working, which made hard work for his fireman. Fireman Doug Holden said that while proceeding up the gradient from Evercreech New to Shepton Mallet you could not reach a sufficiently high speed to get it compounding. However, leaving Shepton you could get it compounding in the dip before Charlton Viaduct and it would compound to Masbury and probably reach there in 'under time' and make life easier for the fireman because it used less steam than other engines.

Compound No. 1053 was reputed to have had larger diameter driving wheels and certainly had a rail round its tender to enable it to carry more coal, but had a smaller water-carrying capacity. This latter feature was a drawback on the 10.15 p.m. Bath to Leicester Parcels run as there was no column at the Leicester end of Birmingham New

A Bournemouth West to Sheffield train leaves Bath hauled by Gloucester-allocated Class 4P Compound No. 41144.

17.8.57 Hugh Ballantyne

Street station. Another fireman claimed that the Compounds were 'diabolical', that they could not compound over the S&D and that older drivers used to keep them working 'simple' even over the relatively level road from Mangotsfield North Junction of Gloucester. Incidentally, the 10.15 p.m. Parcels was known to the Midland men who took over at Birmingham as 'The Rabbits' because rabbits from the heaths around Poole were strung in some of the vans. They would come up to a Bath crew and ask 'Are you "The Rabbits"?'

THE EX-SOMERSET & DORSET CLASS 7F 2-8-0S

The first half-dozen S&D Class 7F 2–8–0s had tender cabs to avoid the need to install larger turntables because at low speeds tender-first working was deemed acceptable. Firemen considered the tender cabs a nuisance as they restricted the use of fire irons. The tender cabs were inclined to collect fumes in tunnels and be draughty in the open. All cabs of this type were removed by December 1920. As a weak underbridge near the entrance to Bath motive power depot precluded them using the facilities there until the bridge was strengthened, they had their fires cleaned in a siding near the gas works. Initially the 7Fs home shed was Radstock.

The first of the S&D Class 7F 2–8–0s, No. 80, at Derby in photographic grey livery. She eventually became British Railways No. 53800.

1914 Author's collection

S&D Class 7F 2–8–0 No. 53809 approaching Chilcompton with an Up goods.

14.8.59 Author

Even after passing through Derby works for an overhaul they retained their characteristics, No. 53808 being the best and No. 53809 the worst. Fred Holmes, running foreman at Bath, held the opinion that the 1914 batch of 2–8–0s with smaller boilers (the G9AS pattern as fitted to 4–4–0 Compounds) steamed better than the 1925 batch, which carried non-standard G9BS boilers 7 in larger in diameter than the G9AS. He believed that they 'didn't seem on top of the job'. Conversely, Fred Epps thought that the larger boiler version was more capable of carrying out the job. Incidentally the 1925 engines had left-hand drive whereas the first batch had right-hand drive.

No. 13809 was fitted with steam sanding gear and this was a nuisance because its control was situated just below the brake control valve and water dripped from the steam sander valve on to the driver's leg. Driver George Prentice had her on one occasion during the Second World War; she was rough riding, would not steam and when George turned the sanders on, the hot water squirted down his legs and the wet sand failed to come out of the boxes. As they drew to a halt at the home signal at Bath Junction he exclaimed: 'I ain't going to have no more from this 'un.' So saying, he caught hold of the coal pick and 'bang', he gave the steam valve a mighty blow. Other engines of the class had dry sanding gear operated by the fireman rattling backwards and forwards a lever protruding through the cab floor. It was efficient unless the sand became wet. You had to

S&D Class 7F 2–8–0 No. 13809 at Masbury Summit, having assisted in the rear a train hauled by a sister engine.

23.7.37 H.C. Casserley

remember to use sand sparingly, or you could quickly use all the sand in the boxes which were cleaned out about twice weekly.

The back sanders always seemed wet, probably due to the cab floor being watered and when going tender-first up an incline, if the back sand failed to emerge, a trick was to put the pet pipe into it and wash the sand down. The sand would not last long using this method, but sometimes it was the only means of gaining adhesion.

Bill Rawles was driving No. 53806 from Evercreech Junction to Bath with Dave Massey firing. He started with sixty-six empty wagons and was assisted to Binegar by a banker which was taken off there, as were six wagons because the reception siding at Bath could only accommodate sixty. Proceeding from Radstock to Midford was rather a struggle and as he approached the latter, Bill asked David, 'All right?' 'Ah,' was the laconic reply. Hearing this, Bill gave No. 53806 full regulator. Midford Bank gradually slowed down the 7F and a quarter of a mile inside Combe Down Tunnel No. 53806 slipped to a standstill. Conditions were unpleasant and metal seemed almost red-hot. Two cattle wagons were next to the engine and the cows in them were bellowing their objections.

Bill set back to the tunnel mouth where he was able to use the lineside phone to contact Percy Savage at Midford signal-box. Percy asked, 'What's the trouble?' Bill explained the situation and Percy said that it was alright to return down to Midford and arranged a bank engine to come out from Bath and pilot No. 53806. Even with the aid of an assisting

The two types of S&D Class 7F 2–8–0 compared. On the right is large boiler No. 53806 and on the left small boiler No. 53802 at Bath MPD. The 'Boat Road' is in the background on the right.

19.3.55 Revd Alan Newman

engine they experienced trouble ascending the gradient. On arrival at Bath, Bill tested the sand and found that although it was working perfectly when he left Evercreech Junction, *en route* the sand had become wet and so failed to fall down and aid adhesion.

Driver Bill King had a similar experience. One day in 1942 he had No. 13809 (now preserved at the Midland Railway Centre, Butterley) to work 'The Market', as the 3.50 p.m. Bath to Evercreech Junction goods was called. No. 13809 travelled for miles without Fireman John Stamp needing to turn on the injector, in fact he double-checked the water level by means of the taps in case the gauge was making a false reading. Only 1,500 gallons were used from Bath to Evercreech Junction instead of the normal consumption of something in excess of 2,500 gallons.

On arrival at Evercreech Junction at about 7.30 p.m. they shunted, turned the engine and proceeded to the passenger station to fill the tank. John trimmed the coal in the tender while Bill had a glass of cider in the public house opposite. Weather permitting it was customary for them to sit on the platform and enjoy their supper of bread, cheese and onions, or if the weather was inclement they ate in the cab. When the signal arm fell they ran No. 13809 to the goods yard where their train back to Bath had already been prepared. On Mondays to Fridays they took a load of sixty empty coal wagons, but no empties were taken on Saturdays. This particular Saturday their load was twenty-six wagons of ammunition.

S&D Class 7F 2–8–0 No. 53809 climbs the 1 in 50 out of Bath with the Bath to Templecombe freight.

21.5.52 R.E. Toop

After the last Up passenger train had cleared the section they left Evercreech Junction at 10.10 p.m. It was a very cold night in January, the moon was full and the ground sparkled with frost. All went well and as soon as John Stamp observed that the Midford distant signal was 'off', he used his pricker to level the fire as he knew that it would not be necessary to add any more coal. He oiled the runner of the tablet catcher, pushed it out before reaching Midford signal-box and shortly afterwards retrieved the caught tablet.

Halfway through Combe Down Tunnel disaster struck. No. 13809's safety valves blew off and she started priming and the floods of water from the chimney caused her to slip on the 1 in 100 rising gradient. Superheated steam poured back into the cab because the water caused more steam than the normal exhaust. Driver King closed the regulator. The steam scalded the fireman severely and when the engine's speed had reduced to about 10 mph, John Stamp jumped off. Driver Bill King stopped the engine and by this time conditions had improved somewhat and John was able to regain the cab. The water was now out of sight in the glass.

Bill opened the regulator, but the condensation of steam on the rails caused No. 13809 to slip. Eventually he succeeded in getting her moving. John always fired with his sleeves rolled up and when at last they emerged from Combe Down Tunnel into the cold, moonlit Lyncombe Vale he realised how badly scalded he was. On both arms all the skin from the finger tips to elbows had come off and his face was blistered. Driver King had not escaped

Whitaker's tablet apparatus on the tender of No. 53809 in Woodham's scrapyard.

1966 C. Steane

The turntable at Evercreech Junction.

6.3.66 C. Steane

The water crane at Evercreech Junction.
February 1966 C. Steane

injury – his hands were so badly burnt that he could not bear to use them and applied the brake with his elbow. As John's hands appeared to be in reasonable condition, although later they peeled, he was able to use the tender handbrake to help control the descent.

Bath Junction home signal was at danger and when they drew to a halt, Bill said to John, 'Go to the signal-box and get him to ring for an ambulance.' John carried the token with him to the box and on reaching it had to tap on the door with his elbow as his hands were too painful to allow him to use them to turn the door handle.

The 'dolly' on the junction signal was pulled off and Driver King brought the train down to the signal-box for his fireman to get on. He drove to the end of the running loop at the approach to Bath goods yard and they were met by a relief driver and fireman from the depot. Bill and John were unable to climb down the steps from the footplate as their hands were too badly burned to grasp the handrails. A step ladder was found to help their descent. An ambulance took them to the Royal United Hospital, where they stayed for ten days. The burns to the fireman's face were so severe that he was unable to shave for a week. Both men were off work for seven weeks.

Bath Junction signal-box.

c. 1966 C. Steane

The water softener being installed at Bath.
1938 Author's collection

S&D Class 7F 2–8–0 No. 53809 about to enter the Chilcompton Tunnel with a Down express.
8.8.59 R.E. Toop

Foreman Tom Rudd ordered No. 13809 to be taken to the shed, its fire dropped and the boilersmith blew the boiler down to eject all the steam. At about 3.00 a.m. George Adams, head fitter, was sent for to seal the blowdown valve and remove it. Harry Whitaker, District Locomotive Superintendent, sealed the valve in a box and despatched it to Derby for examination where it was found to be in order.

Blacksmith Albert Manley examined the flexible pipe between the engine and tender and found it was blocked, thus preventing the escape of water from the blowdown valve. This meant that salts in the boiler water, which had been supplied from the Bath water softener, had become more and more concentrated. Although No. 13809's boiler had been washed out four days previously, the salts had become so concentrated that they caused priming.

The authorities took such care examining the blowdown valve because they were currently tightening up on the 'nobbling' of blowdown valves, which could be rendered non-operational by the insertion of a boot stud. Crews 'nobbled' them in order to save water. For example, if you had on the Bath to Leicester Parcels train a 'Black Five', which was known to use a lot of water, you were faced with a problem. You needed 1,500 gallons in the tank on arrival at Birmingham New Street in order to reach the troughs at Tamworth, but there was no water available on the road used at New Street. The only solution was to fit at Gloucester a blank-ended nut on the blowdown discharge pipe and save about 1 to 1½ gallons every minute.

Instead of continuous blowdown valves being fitted on BR Standard Class 4 and Class 5 engines, a lever was provided on the fireman's side of the cab and when pulled hard, blew down into a pit. A sample of water was taken and tested to discover how concentrated the salts were. Some Bulleid Pacifics had blowdown valves worked by a clock and sealed by the locomotive superintendent. These blew so strongly for 45 seconds that occasionally ballast was blown up and injured people on a nearby platform. In due course the clocks were removed and the engines blown down at a locomotive depot.

If a blowdown valve was not working, deposits on boiler-tubes formed far more rapidly and made an engine less efficient as the heat from the firebox could not raise steam so effectively. To prevent a repetition of the accident to No. 13809, all LMS engines were modified so that the blowdown pipe discharged into the ashpan instead of beside a guard iron at the rear of a tender.

One day Harry Starkey was firing to Fred Holmes on No. 13809. They were working either the 3.30 a.m. or 5.00 a.m. goods from Bath and called at Radstock for banking assistance. They had just reached the north portal of Chilcompton Tunnel when they heard a terrific 'bang' and No. 13809 heeled over. They had always claimed that bankers did not do much work, but the one present on this occasion most certainly did. It thrust the train and engine right into the tunnel.

Large boiler No. 53808 hauling a heavy freight train up the gradient of 1 in 50 through Lyncombe Vale towards Combe Down Tunnel.

21.8.51 Author

Class 7F 2–8–0 No. 53807 at Bath MPD in front of the water softener.

c. 1960 R.J. Cannon/Author's collection

The trouble on No. 13809 was caused by the gudgeon pin nut which came off. The nut should have been retained by a cotter pin, but this must have sheared off and allowed the gudgeon pin nut to turn. The gudgeon pin held the connecting rod to the slipper block which moved backwards and forwards between the slide bars. The front of the connecting rod, now adrift, pushed against the ground and thrust the engine over and had it not been supported by the tunnel brickwork, would have turned right over on its side. Because No. 13809 had been working hard, it had a big fire. As this was no longer needed, the injectors were put on to fill the boiler. Owing to the darkness it could not be seen if the injectors were working, so Harry Starkey got down to feel if they were. The fire was damped down ready for the engine to be rerailed in due course.

On one occasion Jack Barber was driving an ex-works Class 7F when a cylinder head blew out at Midsomer Norton. The cause was found to be a small hammer and chisel that someone at Derby had left in the cylinder. On another occasion Driver Harold Burford played a trick on Jack Barber. The turntable at Evercreech Junction was operated by the driver pushing on one side and the fireman pushing on the other. One night, unknown to Jack, Harold had stopped pushing and crept into some nearby bushes. When Jack passed him pushing the engine, he sprang out with a terrifying roar.

Driver Fred Epps said that the Class 7Fs were so good that he had climbed through Masbury with only 100 lb of steam and forty empty wagons behind – 'They'd battle on – they were wonderful engines.' The fire needed to be deep at the back and shallow at the front for if you threw coal down under the brick arch, the fire became choked.

No. 53807 at Bath MPD. 'Bath's Best' is chalked on the smokebox door hinge. BR Standard Class 5
No. 73082 *Camelot* is on its left.

27.3.64 Revd Alan Newman

THE BULLEID LIGHT PACIFICS

Probably just before March 1951 Driver Ron Gray acted as pilotman on the first 'West Country' Class Pacific to work over the Somerset & Dorset. Bournemouth was playing Bristol City in a football cup match and five specials ran from Bournemouth to Bristol. Ron Gray went to Broadstone to conduct the Southern Region driver over the S&D. At Evercreech Junction he suggested to the driver that it would be a good idea to stop and fill up the water tank before the climb over the Mendips, which they did. There was not much coal in the tender, but the fireman, who had not travelled over the line before, remarked, 'It's alright, there's not much further to go.' The distance to be travelled was only 26 miles, but it included a climb to 811 ft above sea level. The Pacific's wheels lost adhesion which meant that half an hour was added to the scheduled time over the distance of 5 miles, mainly at 1 in 50. The driver of Class 2P 4–4–0 No. 502 acting as pilot had to have his engine in full forward gear. They stopped to raise steam at Shepton Mallet and arrived at Bath forty-five minutes late.

'West Country' Class Pacific No. 34042 *Dorchester* descends into Bath.

28.6.51 Author

On 19 March 1951 'Battle of Britain' Pacific No. 34109 *Sir Trafford Leigh Mallory* was tried over the S&D following the transfer in February 1950 of the locomotive depots to the Southern Region. The SR hoped to use these Light Pacifics to replace 'Black Fives' on loan from the London Midland Region. No. 34109 started with a seven-coach semi-fast and ended with the ten-coach 'Pines Express'. Unaided it only just managed this, so to allow for adverse conditions, its load was set at 270 tons, the same as a 'Black Five'. Although nominally more powerful, the Pacifics lacked adhesion, although Len West claimed that the Pacifics did not slip if handled correctly. If you had your eye on the steam chest pressure gauge and kept the needle below 90, they would rarely slip, but if over this mark, they would slip severely.

The Pacifics were heavy on coal and sometimes consumed so much that there was insufficient in the tender to run from Bath to Bournemouth West and back and so piloting was necessary from Radstock. A criticism of the machines was that the brake was in front of the driver's rather small window and obstructed his view. On rebuilt engines the view was partly obscured by the regulator rod running along the side of the boiler. Their steam reversing gear could cause problems and when shortening the cut-off, it sometimes went into back gear. The trouble lay with the fitters at Bath shed and after they were shown that the reversers needed lubricating, the situation improved. One driver claimed that on the 'Tin Lizzies' the sanders often failed to work through water

Ex-S&DJR Class 4F 0–6–0 No. 44557 pilots 'West Country' Class Pacific No. 34041 *Wilton* near Wellow on the 4.20 p.m. Bath to Bournemouth West.

21.6.58 Author

running down their sides and getting into the sandboxes. On the curves between Wellow and Writhlington they slipped at 60 to 70 mph. Another grumble was that no water gauge was provided on the tender, only cocks for testing the level.

No. 34042 *Dorchester* was considered a very bad steamer. One morning Driver Fred Epps and Fireman Sam Stainer booked on at 2.30 a.m. to work one of the summer Saturday trains to Bournemouth West. On arrival at the engine board at Bath and learning that they had been allocated *Dorchester*, Sam said, 'Never mind.' They set off from Bath with 250 lb on the clock – a full head of steam. By the time they had covered 1¼ miles, about half of it up a gradient of 1 in 50, the gauge had fallen to 180. They managed to reach the mouth of Combe Down Tunnel, the head of the descent to Midford, with 'water winking in the bottom of the glass'. On the return journey they were so short of coal due to *Dorchester*'s voracious appetite, that Sam had to sweep coal forward from the back of the tender. This meant that by the time they reached Bath, Sam had shovelled about 5 tons of coal over the distance of 143 miles. Fred admitted that the Light Pacifics were marvellous runners – you could close the regulator and they would run for miles, and one driver even claimed that they ran faster with the regulator closed. Fred considered the rebuilt engines superior to the original version.

Class 2P 4–4–0 No. 40563 and *Sir Trafford Leigh Mallory* leave Bath with the Down 'Pines Express'.

24.3.51 Hugh Ballantyne

One drawback with the Pacifics was that because the footplate was high, there was very little headroom. Len West was 5 ft 6 in tall and his head touched the roof in places, so it was even more uncomfortable for a tall driver. Dennis Thorne believed that the Pacifics would burn rubbish in the corners of the firebox, but needed good coal under the arch and towards the front.

When the 2.45 a.m. Mail Bath to Bournemouth West was worked by a Pacific it 'slipped like billy-o' on the bank out of Bath, while one driver claimed that with three spots of water on the rails you could not get them up to Masbury. A Pacific used thirty pints of oil when being prepared and then wasted most of it, spilling it out traversing sharp curves; a Midland engine only required four pints. Because the Pacifics had the propensity to slip, a fireman might need as many as ten buckets of sand to fill the boxes.

It was considered that the Bulleid Pacifics had the edge over the 'Black Fives' in terms of better steaming, convenience of controls, comfort, protection from the weather and also because they were equipped with electric lights. On the Mendips it was not infrequent for the wind to blow out the gauge and head lamps. An unlit head lamp would cause a signalman to stop a train and then, because of the wind you could not light it, or them – because often both head lamps were blown out – and this would result in having to bring the lamps back into the shelter of the cab to get them burning again.

THE SOMERSET & DORSET 0–4–0 SENTINEL SHUNTING ENGINES

Towards the end of the 1920s, the small shunting engines low enough to pass beneath the 10 ft 6 in high 'Marble Arch' or 'Tyning Bridge' at Radstock, were nearing the end of their economic life. Looking around for a replacement, Sentinel 0–4–0 shunters were believed to be suitable. They had a vertical boiler situated in the cab and the wheels were coupled by a chain. The vertical cylinders were set towards the front of the engine under a bonnet. The square windows gave an excellent view for shunting. Although the intention was for them to be worked by one engineman who would have done both driving and firing, in actual practice they had a normal crew of two. Most of the repairs and examinations were carried out by the fitter at Radstock shed, but occasionally they ventured as far as Bath or Bristol MPDs when a larger overhaul was required.

As they were designed for shunting, if travelling any distance they soon grew short of steam and running them from Barrow Road Bristol to Radstock was quite an undertaking. Their maximum speed was only about 4 mph. You travelled from Barrow Road to Fishponds and then went into a siding to get up steam. Having achieved this you continued on to Bitton to raise steam in a siding there before moving on to Bath, which was the end of a day's work. Next morning the Sentinel was taken to Radstock, Midford siding being the first stop to raise steam. While waiting for the steam pressure gauge to rise, to enliven a rather dull day, Driver 'Prickle' Thorne placed an inverted bucket on the chimney of a permanent way hut in which men were gathered. They

Sentinel 0–4–0 No. 7191 at Radstock.

5.9.49 S.W. Baker

Sentinel No. 47191 71G at Radstock, its home shed.

26.2.53 Revd Alan Newman

An unidentified Sentinel shunter from Radstock at Bristol, Barrow Road shed. Class 3F 0–6–0 No. 43444 is in the foreground and Class 5 2–6–0 No. 42764 in the background.

c. 1960 R.J. Cannon/Author's collection

The north portal of Wickwar Tunnel.

c. 1900 W.H. Short

came out like enraged bees, but fortunately the signalman chose that moment to pull off the ground dummy and Thorne and the Sentinel were able to make their escape.

One day Driver Mac Woodward and Fireman Fred Epps travelled 'on the cushions' to Stonehouse to accompany Senior Footplate Inspector George Arkwright who was taking a Sentinel shunter to Bath. He had driven it down from Derby after 'shopping' and when the pair met him he was 'as black as the ace of spades'. Arkwright did the driving and Mac was there to pilot him over the road, while Fred carried out a little firing.

The small firebox was down low in a corner and therefore awkward to fire. It took them about eight hours to cover the 34 miles between Stonehouse and Bath. They had to stop four times for water and at stations where there was no column they had to form a chain gang with a bucket. The final time they did this was at Bitton, where a porter and another man assisted the three footplate crew. Fred recalled, 'Oh, it was a terrible thing that, I'll never forget it. The fire was dirty – we got some clinker out of it, but it was difficult to keep steam. We were going more or less block to block and then "inside" to get more steam and fill the boiler up. We just about made it up the gradient and through Wickwar Tunnel and were most thankful to arrive back at Bath.'

INDEX